Young Dressmaker

Young Dressmaker

Margaret J. Heafield

B.T. Batsford Ltd, London

ISBN 0 7134 0584 8

Typeset by Tek-Art Ltd, Kent
and printed in Great Britain by
The Anchor Press Ltd,
Tiptree, Essex
for the publishers
B.T. Batsford Ltd,
4 Fitzhardinge Street
London W1H 0AH

Contents

Dresses

Shawls and capes

Bags

Soft toys and table linen

Acknowledgments

When I wrote this book for young dressmakers of slender means, I had just completed many years of teaching art, creative embroidery and dressmaking, and I would like to thank all the friends, relatives, ex-colleagues and ex-pupils, who helped with it, one way or another. Particular thanks to Mr John Wood, Head of Madeley High School who allowed me (although I was no longer a member of his staff) to borrow the school premises, school equipment and some of my ex-pupils. Also, to Mr Tim Denning, Head of Science who cheerfully gave us his free time to do the photography: to Mrs Beryl Moss of the Art Department who saved me so much time on the drawings; to Carolyn Heafield, Annette and Isobel Titeux, Joanna and Nessie Denning, Beverley Dickin, Julie Carter and Pamela Wakelin, who individually or collectively gave much down-to-earth advice, and made many helpful suggestions, in addition to spending many tedious hours acting as tailor's dummies, dressmaker's apprentices, and finally models. Not forgetting Joyce Richardson who managed to decipher my handwriting and translate it into readable typescript. Finally, my thanks to Thelma M Nye for her advice, guidance and encouragement, without which I would never have thought of up-dating the results of past years' labours and putting them into a book.

Introduction

This book is for all girls who love to have lots of new clothes but who cannot afford to buy them ready-made, and who already know the basic processes of dressmaking, or, at least, can refresh their memories from a needlework book in a public library. If you pale at the price of the two or three sheets of stamped tissue paper known as commercial patterns, if you have a few ideas of your own, if you can follow very simple, step-by-step instructions and do not mind spending a little time beforehand on making your own patterns, then, with the help of this book, you can make almost any garment you like, for a fraction of the price it would cost in the shops.

I collected teenage opinions from the U.S.A., Australia, France and Italy, as well as from girls in the U.K., to give me an international view of the contents of the ideal wardrobe. They were surprisingly similar, the only real differences being due to climatic variations. Even more surprising to me was the restrained, even conservative, choice of garments and styles. However, it is the individual details and the variations on a basic theme that make that mysterious thing called 'fashion'.

This book is a natural progression of a system of integrated patterns, to make any garment in any size, that I have built up over many years of teaching dressmaking. It is a collection of basic patterns which can be varied according to personal taste or the dictates of fashion. They have all been made up to fit girls of various shapes and sizes, to ensure that they work, and have been scaled down in order to fit as many as possible into this book. At the same time, in order to simplify the making of each garment, I have tried to remove every process that was not absolutely necessary. The young dressmaker should, therefore, find the patterns quick and straightforward to follow.

All the different styles of skirts, bodices, sleeves, necklines, collars, etc., will be found here and, because the patterns are all interchangeable, you can make them up in any combination.

Commercial paper patterns, expensive though they are, seldom fit without some adjustment. The same may apply here, but it is usually quite simple to correct the pattern piece and, once this has been done, it can be stored away in your 'library' for future use. The average measurements I have used here are 34–24–34in. (87–61–87cm) and 5ft 3in. (1.68m) tall. For the purpose of this book these have all been metricated.

It should be made clear to any girl using this book at school that some of the short cuts might not be acceptable to examiners and should not be employed if you are making garments for course work such as C.S.E. or G.C.E. 'O' Level. This book is not aimed at examination candidates, but rather at all young needlewomen who want only to make their own simple, attractive, well-fitting clothes cheaply and without too many technical complications. Mothers making clothes for teenagers in the family will find it just as useful and, since many of the garments are classical styles, they may well wish to adapt them for themselves.

Apart from the pleasure of dressing well and inexpensively, the young dressmaker has an almost unlimited choice of fabrics, colours, designs, sizes and styles. No shop, not even the most exclusive boutique, can give you this choice. Furthermore, there is a feeling of great satisfaction in achieving something of, and on, your own. The envious looks of less enterprising friends are a bonus, but take care, or you could find yourself making clothes for them too! Far better to try converting them to this easy, useful and rewarding hobby.

Fashion for every occasion

The basics

This book assumes you know how to put on a patch pocket, a waistband or cuff, a collar or facing; that you can put in a sleeve and a zip fastener; that you can sew a dart properly; that you know the common seams and hems, can put on a bias binding and work a buttonhole by hand and machine. If you are uncertain about any of these processes, there are certain books in your local library from which you can refresh your memory. If you have never come across some of them, it is advisable to try them out with some bits of scrap fabric, rather than risk making mistakes on your new material.

If you are making clothes at school there will be sewing machines, probably very modern electric swing-needle models to use. Take advantage of the zig-zag stitch to neaten very swiftly any seam edges of fabric liable to fray.

If you have a few minutes to spare, and the chance to get hold of one of the instruction books that go with your machines, go through it carefully with the machine in front of you. You will be surprised how much more you can get out of a machine if you really understand it and know how to use it, its attachements and adjustments. Those of you working at home may have the latest model in swing-needle machines, but it is just as likely that you have a reliable, old, hand machine, or even a veteran treadle model. It does not matter what model you use, so long as you know your machine thoroughly. Be sure that the thread and bobbin tensions are correct and that the moving parts are well oiled at all times. I know many people who prefer hand machining because they feel more in control. If you have no access to a machine, or even prefer to work by hand, all of the garments can be made by hand. After all, some of the most elaborate clothes ever worn by men and women were made before sewing machines were invented.

Fabrics and threads

There are so many fabrics for dressmaking nowadays, it is impossible to list them here. Fabrics made from natural fibres – wool, cotton, linen and silk – tend to be more expensive than the extremely wide variety of fabrics made from the many man-made fibres. All have their own virtues and drawbacks, even the clever mixes of natural and man-made fibres. Your choice depends on what you can afford and what you want to make.

For first efforts it is advisable to choose something as cheap as possible. Find out where your nearest open markets are situated. Most sell dressmaking fabrics and also have stalls for cottons, sylkos, elastic, zips, buttons, needles and other haberdashery items, but some markets are better than others so far as choice and price is concerned. On the whole, though, you will find that you will be spoilt for choice, and that you will often pay half the price of the same material from a shop.

Look carefully to see that any fault in the fabric (and sometimes this is why it is sold so cheaply) does not make it impractical to use. Usually, however, the fabrics are the end of a range or bankrupt stock, and are quite perfect. The stall-holder may buy direct from the mill so cutting out the middle-man and he does not have such high overheads as the shop owner. The cottons, sylkos, polyester threads, zips, etc., are similarly much lower in price. Look out also for the stalls where fabrics are piled in untidy, creased heaps, and the haberdashery is thrown haphazardly into boxes. Here you can find the real bargains. For a few pence you can often pick up lengths of material (sometimes expensive stuff) perhaps with a small fault or a dirty mark, that can be avoided when cutting out, or washed out completely. Similar savings can be made in the haberdashery boxes.

Most markets operate on Saturdays, but if the one you would like to patronise is on a weekday, try to think ahead and buy your materials in your holidays or, if you are still at school, persuade your needlework teacher to organise a group visit.

Before you decide what to buy, try to give some thought to what you want from your material. Do you want it to be stretchy and comfortable, soft and easily gathered, crisp and cool, crease-resistant and packable, washable and non-iron, stiff and rustling, warm and light, heavy and hardwearing, exotic and eyecatching, and so on. Always look at and feel all available fabrics before you decide. Get your threads, zips, buttons, bias binding or whatever you need at the same time, and be sure the thread is right for the fabric.

Enlarging the small-scale pattern diagrams

Unless otherwise stated, all the scale patterns in the book are drawn 1 square (5 mm) = 4 cm. If you are still at school, your Needlework Department will have sheets of 1 cm^2 ruled draughting paper. Get a black felt-tipped pen and rule over the line every 4 cm to emphasise the 4 cm squares. The 1 cm divisions are very useful in graduating lines between main points on the patterns. Ready-ruled paper can be bought in craft or stationery shops, but it is very expensive. An alternative is to buy a roll of cheap lining paper and rule if off yourself into 1 cm thin lines and 4 cm thick lines. An even cheaper option is to use newspapers.

Enlarging, using squares, is quite a simple process. With reference to any of the scaled-down patterns, find a convenient place in the top left hand part of the small scale pattern, where the outline of the pattern crosses one of the square lines. From this point, count the number of squares from the top of the pattern and in from the left hand edge of the pattern. Count the same number on the 4 cm squared paper and mark the indentical place. Move along the outline of the small scale pattern, and each time it crosses a square line, mark the identical spot on the large sheet square lines. It sometimes happens that you have to estimate an important point on the pattern that comes *inside* a square. The 1 cm lines help here. Every few squares, join up the dots lightly. The really important thing when enlarging like this, is to be as accurate as possible. Whether the pattern outline crosses the square lines one-quarter or three-quarters, or one-third or seven-eighths of the distance along the edge of the square, it must be as identical as is possible on the enlargement. Here again the light 1 cm lines are a useful guide. When finished, double check, then using a ruler where necessary, outline the pattern with bold black pen lines, ironing out any unwanted dents or bulges, where lines should be straight or smoothly curved. Then mark accurately any notches, numbers and other instructions or information on the pattern piece, and cut out very carefully.

When you have finished using a pattern, fold it and put it in a large labelled envelope or box, to use again. It might also be a pattern or part of a pattern that occurs in another garment, and will not need to be cut again. In this way you can build up your own library of patterns.

Variations

The patterns in this book are designed to integrate one with another, and fit, whatever the combination, so that you could use the sleeves of one with the bodice of another, the skirt of another and the collar of yet another. You might want to turn the shirt into a shirt-dress or the pullover into a T-shirt-dress, by lengthening the shirt or pullover patterns, or make a shortie nightie by shortening the pattern and adding the bikini briefs.

The only patterns that are not totally interchangeable are the two jackets which are slightly larger than the rest so that they can be worn over other outfits.

While putting together one's own variations enables anyone to be a bit different from the rest, the true individual touch that the wealthy pay so much for is more a question of time than money. I make a few suggestions – maybe you can think of others!

Instead of straight hems round skirts, collars, sleeves, etc., make a scalloped or zig-zag hem.
A bold monogram in satin stitch on pocket, yoke or sleeve.
A strip or shape of good lace insertion.
A piece of dainty embroidery or, alternatively, bold embroidery on collar, cuffs, yoke, or hem, or even strips of heavier embroidery inserted, or used as decorative facings.
If you have one of the latest machines that does decorative embroidery, wide bands of this round hems, etc., looks exotic.
Surface top-stitched bands, strapping, or other ornamental details.
Canvas embroidered or hand-woven belts, or other unusual belts or buttons.
Complementary shades of one colour, contrasting colour schemes, or unusual, exotically clashing colour schemes.
Soft, real fur edgings.
Appliqued motifs.

A good Needlework Encyclopaedia will explain how to go about these sort of processes.

Sizing alterations

All the patterns were draughted for the measurements we found to be average for 15 to 25 year olds – height 1.68 m (5 ft 3 in.); bust 87 cm (34 in.); waist 61 cm (24 in.); hips 87 cm (34 in.). Although many of you will be average or near enough to use the average pattern, some of you will be thinner and some will be more well developed.

The standard practice used by dressmaking books and commercial patterns to lengthen or shorten any pattern piece is simple and effective. Look for the double lines across it. Here you either pin in a tuck to shorten, or cut and insert a strip of paper to lengthen.

To reduce or increase the width of the pattern pieces in this book the same method can be used, but certain other adjustments will also have to be made, usually to shoulders and armholes, but occasionally elsewhere. Make sure you check the diagrams carefully for these. *Remember also, that to add to, or take away 5 cm from the average size patterns, all that has to be subtracted from, or added to, each half pattern is 1.25 cm.* If this is all, it is undoubtedly easiest, simply to add it to, or take it from, skirts, bodice or trousers side seams, but if there is more difference than this, please follow the diagrams. Even if you are of average measurements now, you could still make the side seams wider, so that if you do put on weight, you can let out the side seams again. This is a sensible safety precaution, not just being lazy!

The best way to make patterns in different sizes from the average one is as follows. First draw the enlargement of the small diagram accurately on a piece of paper a little larger than the pattern piece. *Do not cut out.* Draw in the vertical and horizontal alteration lines. Cut between them. To enlarge: insert a strip of paper the width required (i.e. quarter of the extra width needed) and sellotape it in place. To reduce: make a tuck, or overlap the edges, and stick. *Re-draw the shoulder line and armhole*, if it is the bodice pattern, because the shoulder will have become too wide or too narrow, and remember that the sleeve may also need

Diagrams showing how to enlarge or reduce the
average size patterns drawn to scale in the book

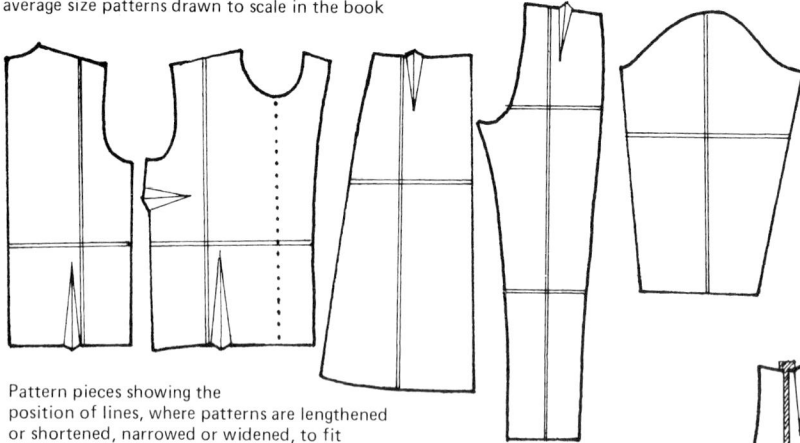

Pattern pieces showing the
position of lines, where patterns are lengthened
or shortened, narrowed or widened, to fit
other than the average measurements

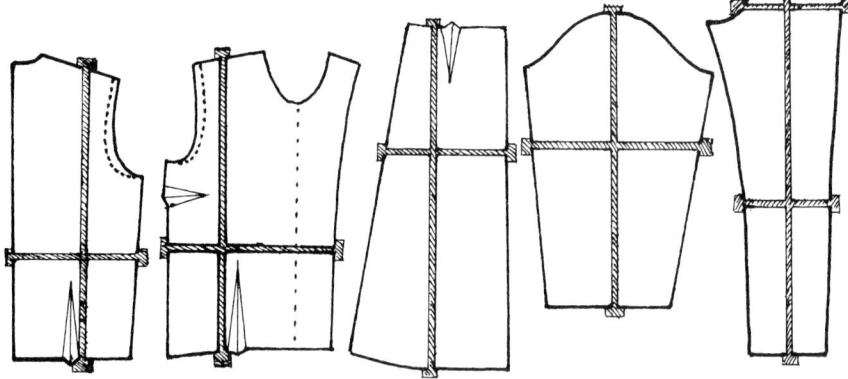

The same pattern pieces showing them, widened and lengthened one size (5 cm) overall, 1.25 cm each piece,
and the adjustment to the shoulder seams and armholes, that is usually, but not always, necessary (dotted lines)

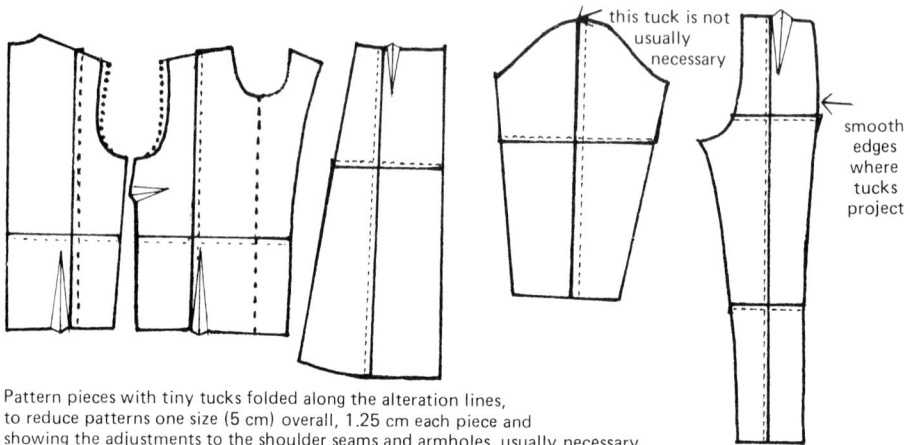

this tuck is not
usually
necessary

smooth
edges
where
tucks
project

Pattern pieces with tiny tucks folded along the alteration lines,
to reduce patterns one size (5 cm) overall, 1.25 cm each piece and
showing the adjustments to the shoulder seams and armholes, usually necessary

widening by the same amount especially at the top where it fits into the armhole. Shorten or lengthen if necessary, then cut out.

Personal patterns

If you enjoy making all your own clothes, you might like to invest in *Betty Foster's Basic Master Pattern* which caters for the more difficult variations of your figure from standard patterns. Including post and packing it is £1.00 from Betty Foster (Fashion Sewing Ltd.), P.O. Box 28, Crewe, Cheshire. Betty Foster is the Radio and Television broadcaster who has brought home dressmaking to thousands with her courses designed for amateurs.

There is also an extremely ingenious method of drafting personal patterns, fitting perfectly, worked out by an Austrian designer, and known as the Lutterloh System. It seems foolproof – very simple yet completely accurate for any figure. Unfortunately, it is rather expensive, unless a group of friends could share one. The Lutterloh System can be obtained from the general distributor, Michael Hawkins, Lutterloh System International, PO Box 3, Coventry, for £34.95, plus £1.35 p & p.

Useful hints for new dressmakers

1 If the fabric is to make a garment that will be washed, and is of cotton or a fabric that is likely to shrink (e.g. denim), wash it and carefully iron it while still slightly damp *before* cutting out the pieces. Sometimes the colours of cheaper, foreign fabrics, particularly brown, black, red or yellow, are liable to 'run' when washed, and washing before making up can save a lot of trouble.

2 For the professional look, press each seam and dart, *as you sew it*, under a damp cloth, and tie off and snip off thread ends. Never join two unpressed seams.

3 Even though you may feel confident enough not to tack seams but to pin instead, it is a good idea to chalk or lightly pencil-in the line for stitching. Put in the pins 1 cm or so on either side of the line to hold the pieces together in position. Then the whole seam can be sewn without stopping to remove pins and will be smoother and more accurate. If there is a tricky join to be made e.g. collar to neck edge, *always* tack it securely. It is well worth the extra minutes.

4 If it is at all possible at school or at home – work with an interested friend. You will both benefit. You can fit and pin up each other's garments, sort out small problems, be critics, give praise and generally bolster each other's self-confidence. If you cannot find a dressmaker's mate, try to get hold of a full length mirror. It is a considerable advantage to be able to see yourself full length, both front and back view in a mirror.

5 Whether you are slim or not, never make your clothes too tight. It is uncomfortable, results in split seams, and looks inelegant. Always allow room for ease of movement. It is a good rule to pin a fairly snug fit, then mark a stitching line about 1.5 cm *outside* the pins (more under arms). The patterns allow for generous 1 cm seams, but it does no harm to have more, and a good hem is useful and gives a better appearance and 'hang'.

6 Always be honest about your real measurements, it simply does not pay to breathe in and measure your waist! If the true measurements do not meet with your approval, it is up to you to do something about them.

7 Recognise any faults in your figure and then try to avoid styles that emphasise them; instead wear designs that disguise them.

8 If you have any garment that is a standard design (e.g. a pair of jeans, a jacket, etc.) that you like, and which fits you well, but which is worn out, do not throw it away; unpick one half of it, carefully wash and press the pieces, and you have an ideal pattern template. Make a note of any detail you unpicked that you may need to be reminded of, and pin it to it.

9 When you have cut out the various pattern pieces in fabric, pin the darts carefully and

closely, then the side seams, etc. Then try on the section and get a helpful friend to correct and adjust the pinned seams to a comfortable fit. Mark pin-positions lightly. Take off the section and follow the marking and pinning advice in Hints 3 and 5. Trim surplus from seams where necessary for even-sized seams. Unpin the pieces, and *immediately* place them on the paper pattern and *correct that also*. Then you will be sure that it is a correct fit when you next come to use it. If you do this very carefully with each part, you can actually make that part of the garment ever after without tedious fitting. *Then, if necessary, before pinning pieces together again to sew, neaten the edges of each piece. It is much quicker and easier to do it now.*

10 If you have any gathering to do (e.g. at waist, cuff or yoke), instead of going to the trouble of changing to the gathering foot, which is frequently inefficient in any case, simply move the stitch-length lever or knob to the longest stitch possible. Sew along the edge to be gathered, leaving an inch or two of the thread at each end. Take hold of the bobbin thread and pull gently from either end until the length required is arrived at. The gathering is beautifully even and can be gently and easily dispersed over whatever length is required. It is also an excellent way to ease one edge into another shorter edge (e.g. the top of sleeves into armholes).

When gathering is permanently machined in place, the threads can be pulled out. If a large area is to be done, as in the bodice of the party dress (*see p. 70*) use a much stronger thread on the bobbin – the strongest you can obtain. We used a fine crochet thread for that dress – a really tough yarn. Some people would gather this type of dress with shirr-elastic, but that is often too weak to gather sufficiently, has to be pulled up, and easily snaps. It also tends to balloon between the lines of elastic, and it rides up. The ready-shirred material that can be bought gives too little fabric in the skirt for a good line. It is much better to do double lines of gathering as described above, which are then pulled up by the strong bobbin threads, to fit

exactly and comfortably, without being hot and clinging, and then are tied off securely either side of the zip or opening.

11 If you are ever brave enough to make clothes in velvet and do not have a velvet board on which to press seams, use a stiff hair or clothes brush under the seams (pile to bristles), a damp cloth on top, gentle pressure and moderate heat.

Note 1 All the work sheets start at the beginning of making up the garment. So think carefully when you lay your patterns on your material. Are the 'on the straight' arrows just that, and the 'place to a fold' edges on a fold? Make full use of your material and *always* put the larger pieces on first and fill up the spaces with the smaller ones. Change them about to be as economical as possible. Take care with fabrics with a pile or a one-way pattern, that all pieces are laid on the *same* and the *right* way. Check and re-check *before* you cut or chalk and cut.

Note 2 Last, and very important: do not panic at the sight of the work sheet instructions. Take one sentence at a time and *do what it says,* before looking at the next.
Good luck!

Aprons

These are the three most popular styles of apron, all simple to make and suitable for beginners and early needlework course work. Apron 1 was made in crisp, cornflower blue and white striped cotton, and the matching cap would make it a useful outfit for the Domestic Science Room at school. Apron 2 was made in printed cotton in autumn colours and bound with brown, and apron 3 was in a brown and yellow print and had a dark brown hem facing and waistband.

1   Traditional cook's apron and cap

See p. 20 for pattern pieces. Press, pin and tack a 2 cm deep hem along the top edge of the pockets. Machine. Press a 1 cm single turning round the other three sides. Place in position on the front of the apron, the small one, top left. Pin, tack and machine. Also mark and stitch the dividing lines in the large pocket. Double stitch the top ends of the seams that take the wear. Pull through the ends to the back, tie off very securely and snip ends neatly.

Take each of the neck straps and waist ties, fold them edge to edge, right sides together. Pin, tack and machine 1 cm from edge. Press seams open. Stitch across one end of each. Using a ruler or cane, push them right side out and press with the seams central.

Starting at the waist edge, apply bias binding, with right sides facing, all the way round the apron. Turn it over, press and stitch it down on

1 Traditional cook's apron and cap

19

1 Traditional cook's apron and cap

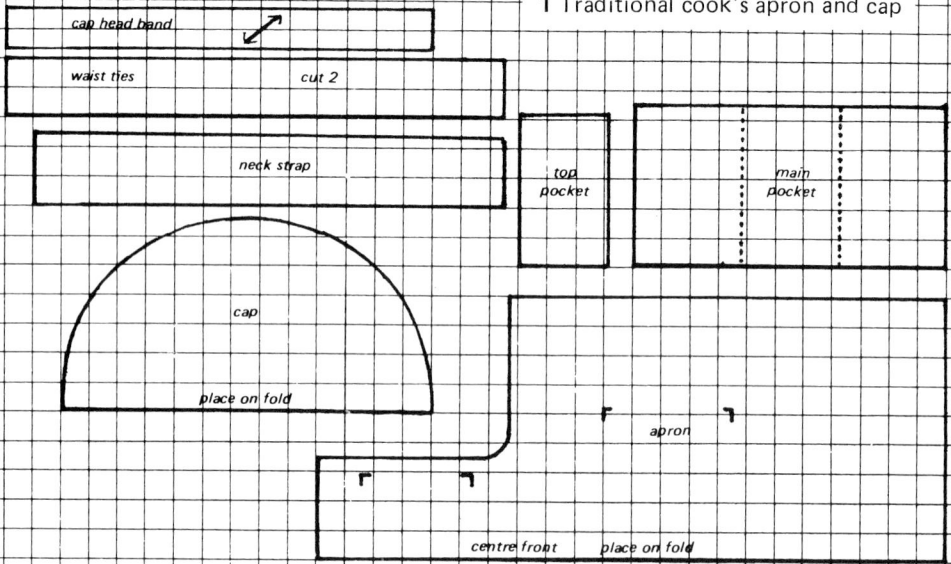

cap head band

waist ties | cut 2

neck strap

top pocket

main pocket

cap

place on fold

apron

centre front | place on fold

3 Classic waist apron

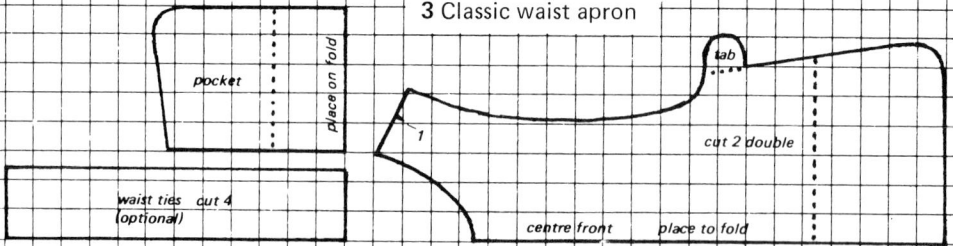

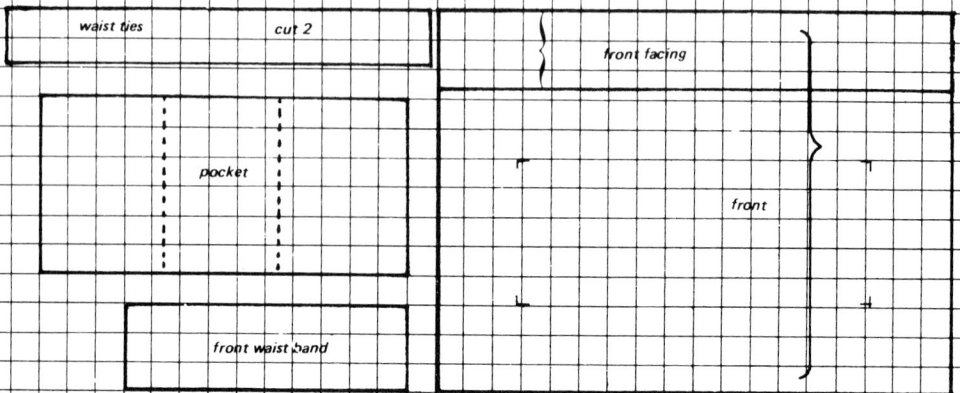

pocket

place on fold

tab

1

cut 2 double

waist ties | cut 4 (optional)

centre front | place to fold

waist ties | cut 2

front facing

pocket

front

front waist band

the wrong side. If you are making the apron to last several years (and want to allow room for growth, both outwards and upwards), instead of binding all the way round, do the two sides only and turn hems at the top and bottom to fit you now. They can be let down when needed.

Pin the waist ties and the shoulder straps into position and stitch on carefully, fastening off securely.

The cap is simply gathered round the edge (as in Hint 10). Try on the headband to fit comfortably and then stitch the ends together. Pin the gathered edge to the headband, with right sides together. Spread gathers evenly, tack and stitch. Press over half the headband to the inside, turn in the raw edge, and stitch. Press. Alternatively, make the band much looser and thread elastic through it, or make a small hem round the cap itself and insert elastic inside it to fit.

2   French cook's apron

See p. 20 for pattern pieces. Bind the top edge of the full-width pocket. Pin into position. Mark, then pin, tack and stitch the dividing lines in the pocket. Reinforce the stitches at the top edge where it takes the wear. Fasten off.

Pin and tack bias binding round entire outer edge (right sides facing). Stitch. Press over half way, pin, tack and stitch on the inside.

Repeat this round the neck edge.

If using the waist tabs, either make a button and buttonhole fastening each side, or sew a small square of Velcro on each tab.

If you prefer waist ties, make the four ties as described in apron 1. Pin them into position, two each side, and stitch very securely. Tie off.

2 French cook's apron

3   Classic waist apron

See p. 20 for pattern pieces. Take the right side of the bottom hem facing and place it to the wrong side of the bottom of the apron. Pin, tack and stitch 1 cm from bottom. Press facing to the right side. Turn down a hem along the top of the facing. Pin, tack and stitch neatly. This is actually a good place for a little decorative embroidery if you want to look different.

Press a small double hem down each side. Pin, tack and stitch carefully.

Press down a good turning at each end of the waistband and also press a crease along the centre.

Gather the top edge of the apron as described in Hint 10, to fit the waistband. Pin, tack and stitch, with right sides together. Press over the waistband, turn in the raw edge to cover the back of the gathers, but before pinning, tacking and stitching, slip the raw ends of the two waist ties into each end of the waistband and pin. When stitching the waistband down at the back, sew across the ends of the waistband too, and tie off very securely.

3 Classic waist apron

Blouses and shirts

Three of the four blouses are straightforward popular styles, with variations in sleeves, collars and pockets. They can be worn in or outside skirt or trousers. If waist darts to fit are preferred, they are simple to pin in and stitch. Blouse 4 was made in a white lacy polyester jersey as a sports shirt; blouse 5 in a tiny blue-and-white checked, non-iron fabric, with a narrow blue velvet ribbon bow at the high neckline. For blouse 6, with the very full sleeves and 'grandad' collar, I was lucky to get a length of beautiful, natural-coloured silk. As this was so soft, the collar, cuffs and front facings needed stiffening slightly; so I used a fine nylon organdy interlining. Always consider this when making up soft or fine fabrics. Blouse 7 was made up with both long and short sleeves. The magyar style is extremely simple with no sleeves to put in, and a very straightforward roll-down collar.

4 Shirt blouse

See p. 24 for pattern pieces. Pin bodice pieces together to check fit, as outlined in Hint 9.

With the knowledge that fraying edges are neatened and all pieces fit, join shoulder edges (notch 1) and side edges (notch 2) following Hint 3. Press seams open and flat. Fold back front facing where pattern indicates, and press. Turn in smaller shoulder seams to match the main ones and hand-hem securely.

Carefully measure bottom hem (I allowed 1 cm single turn and 2 cm double turn). Press,

4 Shirt blouse

4 Shirt blouse **5** High-necked blouse **6** Long-sleeved, high-necked blouse

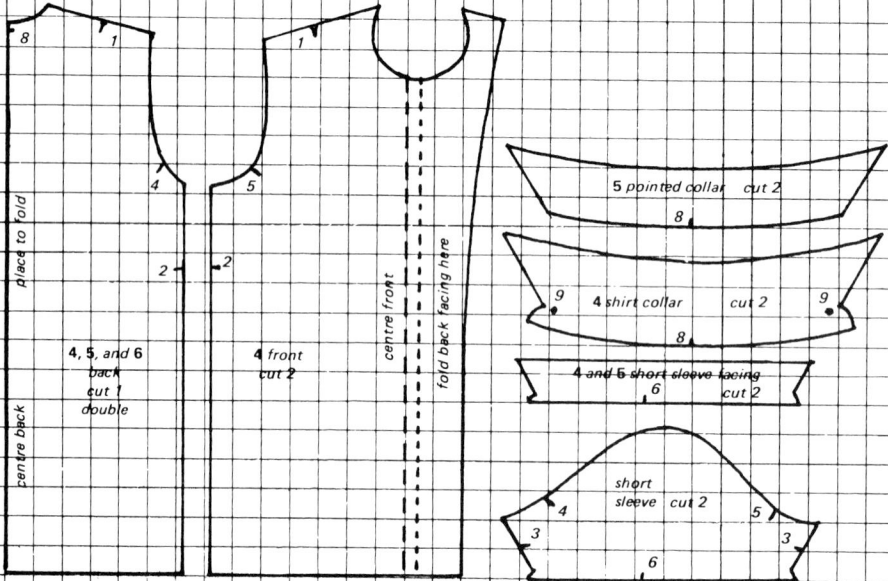

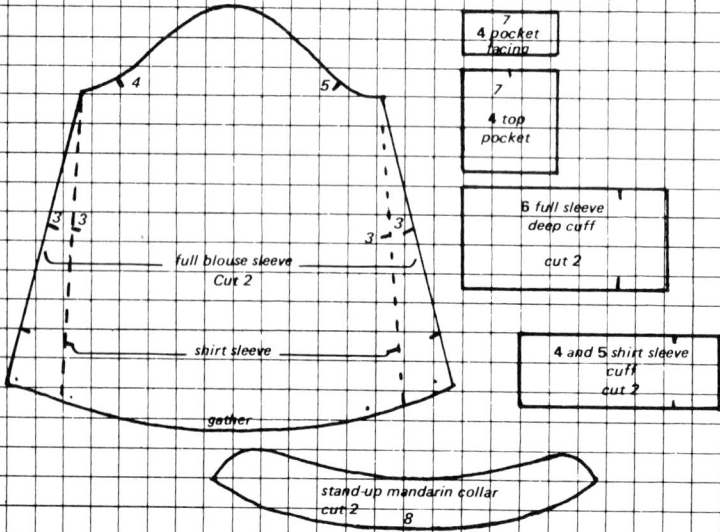

8

1

1

place to fold

centre back

4

5

2

2

4, 5, and 6
back
cut 1
double

4 front
cut 2

centre front

fold back facing here

5 pointed collar cut 2

8

9

4 shirt collar cut 2

9

8

4 and 6 short sleeve facing
6 cut 2

short
sleeve cut 2

4

5

3

3

6

4

5

3

3

3

3

3

3

full blouse sleeve
Cut 2

shirt sleeve

gather

7
4 pocket
facing

7
4 top
pocket

6 full sleeve
deep cuff

cut 2

4 and 5 shirt sleeve
cuff
cut 2

stand-up mandarin collar
cut 2
8

pin and tack in position, but press the hem inside the facing as a single hem to avoid bulk there. Machine carefully to the inner edge of the facings and neaten ends, or slip-stitch by hand. Oversew bottom edges of front and facings together neatly.

Place right side of short-sleeve facings and wrong side of short sleeves together. Pin, tack and machine along bottom edge. Press upwards to the right side of sleeve. Turn in 1 cm, turning at top edge of facing, press, pin, tack and top-stitch carefully. Join sides of sleeves (notch 3). Some prefer to machine and fell here on short sleeves for inner neatness.

Run a line of stitching round top of sleeves as described in Hint 10. Matching underarm seams and notches 4 and 5, pin sleeves into armholes. (Did you check the armholes were big enough, or whether they needed trimming off, when you tried on the bodice at the beginning?) Gently pull the stitching to ease in top of sleeve, to fit the top of the armholes. Tack carefully and stitch. Press seam towards sleeve.

Stitch around edge of the double shirt collar, right sides together. Nick down to stitching at point 9. Turn inside out. Gently poke points and press.

Place the centre right side of one half of collar to the centre back wrong side neck edge of blouse at point 8. Pin. Position collar ends in line with folded edges of front facings and pin. Ease the rest of the collar into neck, tack carefully and stitch. Tie thread ends very securely. Press seam upwards. Clip all round curve of neck edge. Turn in neck edge of the other half of the collar, and pin to stitched seam. Tack, then hand-hem it to the machine stitching. Fasten off securely. Press flat.

Mark positions of buttons and buttonholes. Work buttonholes, re-check button positions and sew on securely.

Note If pockets are required, stitch the ready-made pockets (with facings put on in the same way as the short-sleeve facings) into position, after pressing back the front facings and stitching short shoulder seams.

5 High-necked blouse

See p. 24 for pattern pieces. The instructions are as for blouse 4, but the short blouse collar used does not come to the edges of facings but stops about 3 cm in. So, before pressing back the facings, (*see above*) pin neck edge of blouse and facing with right sides together, and stitch 3 cm in at each end. Tie ends securely. Turn right side out, after nicking the neck edge, down to the last stitch on either side. The collar then fits between the two nicked points, giving either small revers or a small overlap for high-neck fastening.

5 High-necked blouse

6 Long-sleeved, high-necked blouse

See p. 24 for pattern pieces. The instructions are as for blouse 4. However, the short-sleeve facing stage is replaced by gathering wrist edges of shirt-sleeve or full-sleeved blouse, as in Hint 10, measuring your wrist loosely, and putting on the cuff, spreading the gathers along that measurement, and leaving the rest of the cuff as over or under flap. The neck is done as in blouse 4, even though it is a different style.

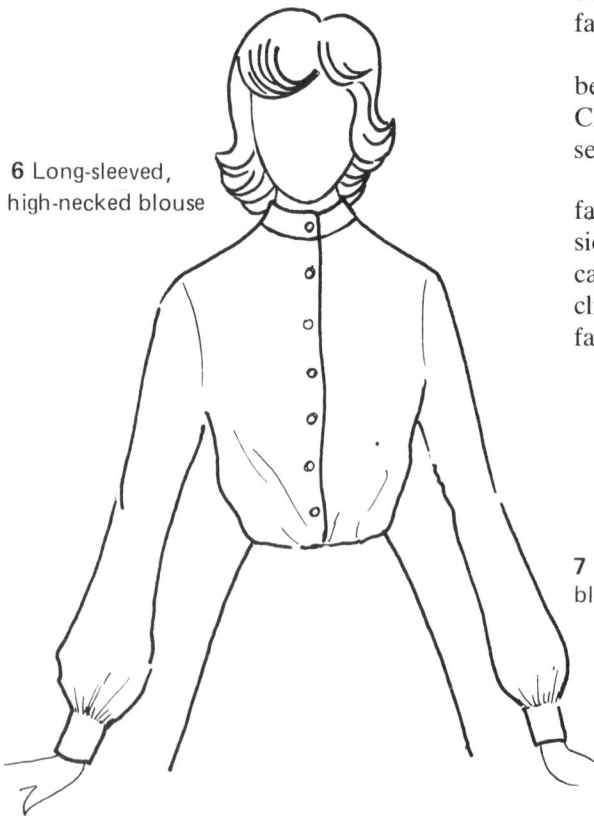

6 Long-sleeved, high-necked blouse

7 Magyar-sleeved blouse

See p. 27 for pattern pieces. Pin and stitch elbow darts. Press. With fronts and back right sides together, pin, tack and stitch from point 5, matching notch 1 to end of sleeve (cap, short or long). Press flat. Nick collar carefully to both notches 5.

Join sides and underarm edges of back and fronts, right sides together. Clip underarm curve. Press flat. Neaten free edges of all facings.

Join centre back collar, and centre back of facings, matching notch 3, nicking carefully to both points 5; also underarm seam of sleeve facings. Press.

Join collar neck edge to blouse neck edge between points 5. Stitch. Tie off ends securely. Clip at intervals along the neck edge and press seam towards outer edge.

For an unbound blouse, apply joined front facings and sleeve facings in the usual way, right sides to right sides; stitch, clip curved edges carefully, turn inside and press. Turn under clipped neck edge and shoulder seams of the facing. Tack and hand stitch to main blouse

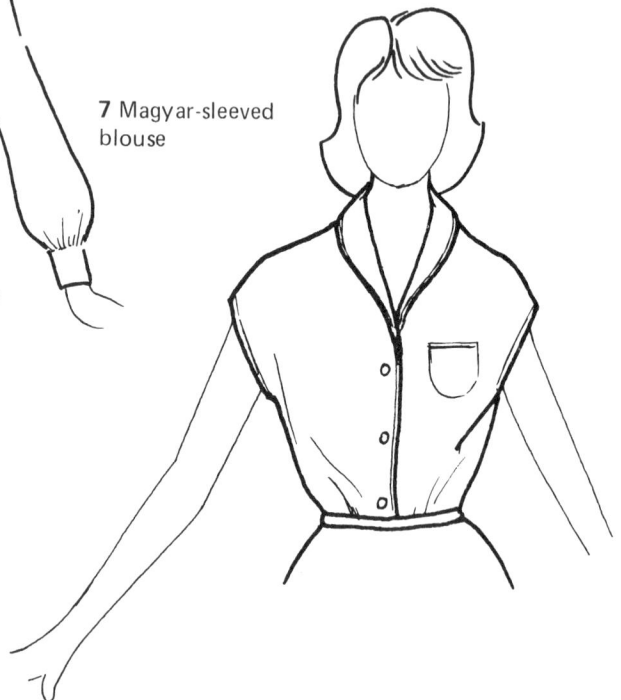

7 Magyar-sleeved blouse

7 Magyar-sleeved blouse

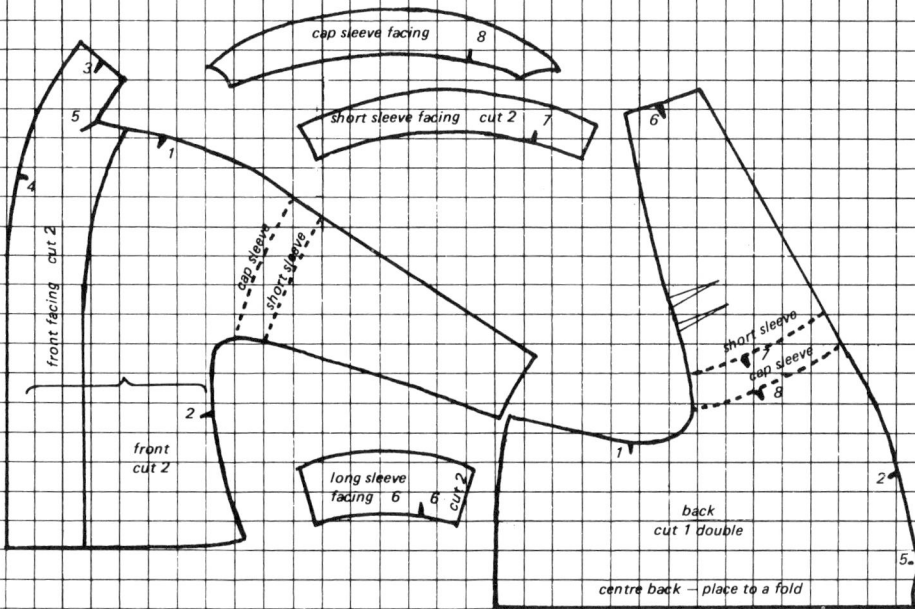

neck and shoulder seams. Press. Complete bottom hem as in blouse 4.

For a blouse with a contrasting colour, pin facings to blouse, wrong sides together, turn up bottom hem as in blouse 4. Bind front and collar edges with contrasting binding. Bind sleeve edges and pocket tops. Stitch pockets in position.

Work buttonholes in the usual way and stitch on buttons.

skirts

The first of this collection of seven skirts, a slim, straight skirt, with optional side or back-seam splits, was made in a heavy-weight, crimpelene-type fabric that would keep its shape and not shrink. The second, a swinging four-gored skirt was made in a dark brown velvet with tiny ivory spots. I also made the bolero (pattern 22 on page 49) in this velvet, to complete an attractive outfit which included the long, full-sleeved 'grandad' collar silk blouse. The softly ra-ra skirt was made from a silky polyester jersey, leopard-skin print, and the flounced ra-ra from a similar, multi-coloured, abstract patterned material. The rhumba skirt was of black and white, printed, stiffish cotton material with each of its three tiers of frills bound with scarlet binding, and the circular skirt in jade green, navy spotted, silky polyester jersey. The wrap-over skirt was made in brown denim for hockey and in white cotton for tennis, and I made the back-belted gilet (pattern 23 on page 51) to go with it, worn over the open-necked shirt blouse on page 25. In fact, all of these skirts (except the rhumba skirt) can be made whatever length you wish, from mini to floor length.

8   Straight skirt

See p. 32 for pattern pieces. Having followed Hint 9, stitch darts in back skirt pieces. Press. Stitch centre back seam (notch 1). Press flat. Stitch front skirt darts. (These are very small

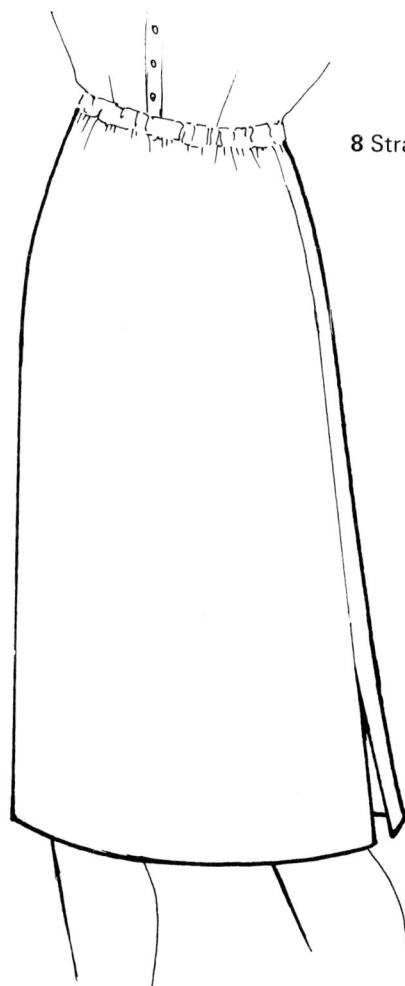

8 Straight skirt

and tapered to mould skirt over hip bones.)
Press. Join back and front together (notches 2).

Note Whichever seams (if any) you want to have
split, leave unstitched to the height required.
Press the facing back into position and pin
down. Leave for the moment.

Carefully unpick 20 cm at the top end of left
side or centre back seam. Tie ends securely and
tack and stitch zip fastener in position.

Machine a line of stitching round waist edge
of skirt 1 cm down, using longest stitch.

Attach waistband, gently easing skirt into
waistband by pulling bobbin thread gently (Hint
10). Stitch on waist fasteners.

Note If you prefer an elasticated waist (which
is very fashionable at the moment) it is much
simpler. No darts or zip are needed. Take a
piece of wide elastic, comfortably fitting your
waist. Join ends securely. Enclose this elastic
waistband in a seam, turned down at the waist
edge of the skirt, the width of the elastic, plus
approximately 7.5 mm. Tack, then zig-zag over
the raw edge for reduced bulk, or, if edge
has already been zig-zag neatened,
a simple straight-stitch will suffice.
'Hollowbacks' may need to adjust
waist level before stitching.

Try on, and get help to mark skirt length. Zig-
zag over raw edge to neaten and slip-stitch into
place. Take care that sides of splits are exactly
level and slip-stitch (and oversew at hem
turning) the pinned facings all round the split,
very invisibly. Press.

9   Four-gored, flared skirt

See p. 32 for pattern pieces. Join two centre
front and two centre back edges (notch 1) then
press. Join side seams (notch 2) and press.

Unpick top left side or centre back seam,
enough to insert zip.

Measure and attach waistband; sew on waist
fastenings.

Try on, level hemline, turn up a very small
hem and top-stitch, or apply soft bias binding as
a narrow hem facing. Press.

9 Four-gored
flared skirt

10 Flounced ra-ra skirt

See p. 32 for pattern pieces. Join side edges (notch 1) of back and front together and press.

Join together the pieces for the flounce (notch 2). Press.

Stitch along top edge of flounce, 1 cm in, on the longest stitch. Pull up as explained in Hint 10 and stroke the gathers evenly.

With right side together, pin the flounce to the body of the skirt (match side seams and centre back and front, then progress all round). Tack. Stitch, and press join in an upward direction, then tack. Top-stitch to anchor the gathered edge inside.

Put in waist elastic as in skirt 8.

Turn up and press a small double hem at the bottom and pin. Tack and stitch. Press.

10 Flounced ra-ra skirt

11 Pleated ra-ra skirt

See p. 32 for pattern pieces. Join side edges of skirt top (notch 1) and press or, if a waistband is desired, stitch front and back darts and press, and then stitch right side seam·and put a 12 cm zip into the left hand side seam, before putting on a waistband.

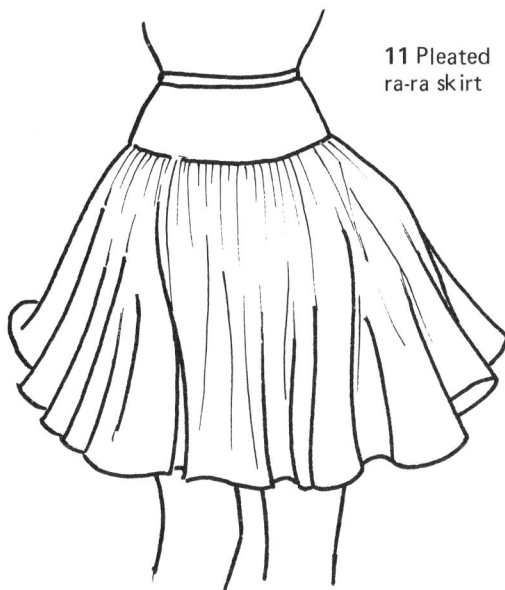

11 Pleated ra-ra skirt

Join the pieces for the pleated part of the skirt (notch 2) and press. Pin a 1 cm pleat (= 2 cm), at 1 cm intervals, around the top edge of the 288 cm length, so reducing it to 96 cm. With right sides facing, pin the 96 cm pleated edge to the 96 cm of the skirt yoke, matching side seams, etc. Tack securely.

Attach in the same way as skirt 10. Try on.

Stitch hem as in skirt 10.

Note If an elasticated waist is required, which is much easier and quicker, follow the instructions in skirt 8.

8 Straight skirt   **9** Four-gored flared skirt
10 Flounced ra-ra skirt   **11** Pleated ra-ra skirt   **12** Wrap-over skirt

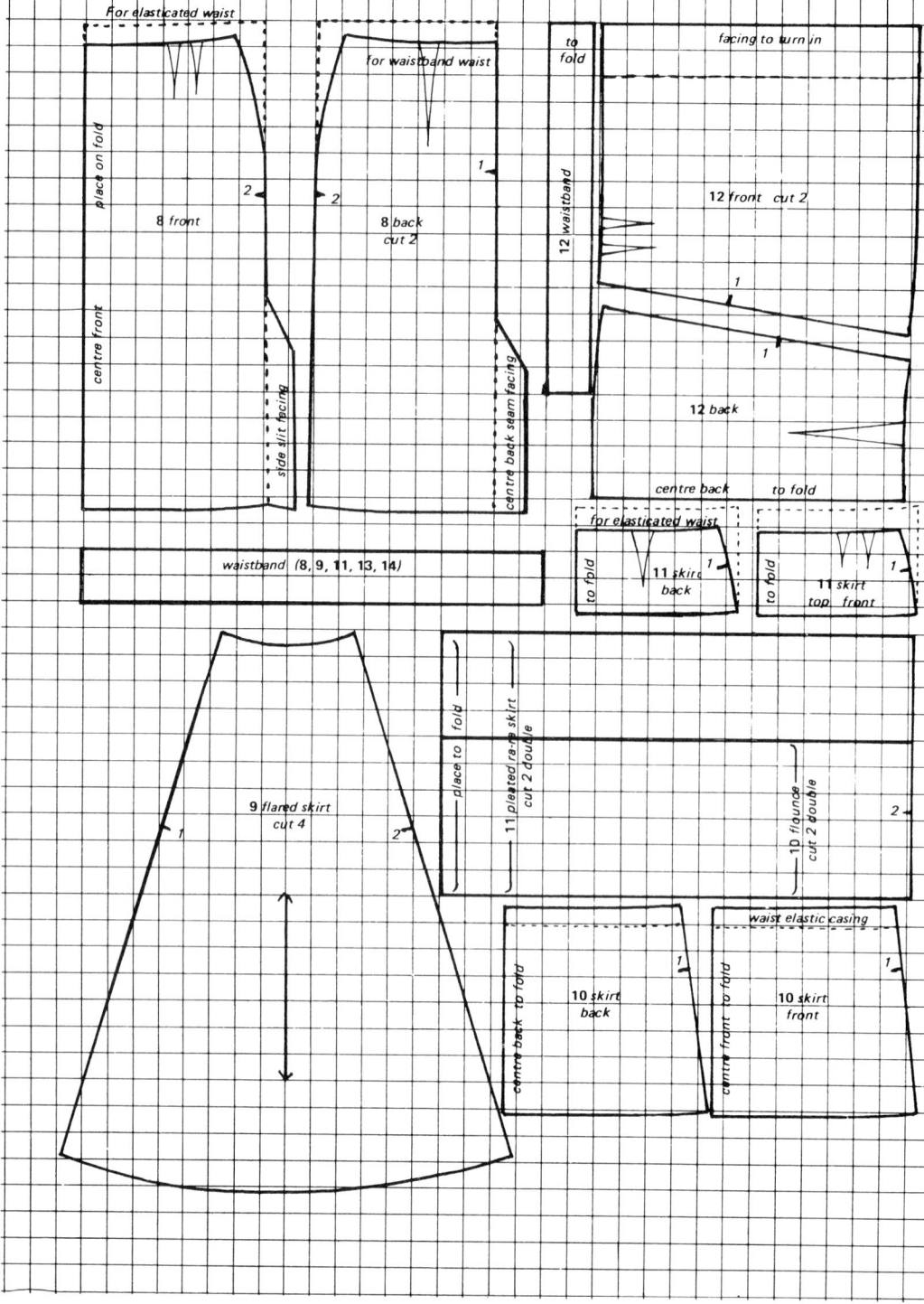

For elasticated waist

for waistband waist

to fold

facing to turn in

place on fold

1

2 ◄   2

8 front

8 back
cut 2

12 waistband

12 front   cut 2

centre front

1

1

12 back

side slit facing

centre back seam facing

centre back   to fold

For elasticated waist

waistband (8, 9, **11**, 13, 14)

to fold

11 skirt
back

1

to fold

11 skirt
top   front

1

place to   fold

11 pleated ra-ra skirt
cut 2 double

10 flounce
cut 2 double

2 ◄

1

9 flared skirt
cut 4

2 ◄

centre back   to fold

10 skirt
back

1

centre front   to fold

waist elastic casing

10 skirt
front

1

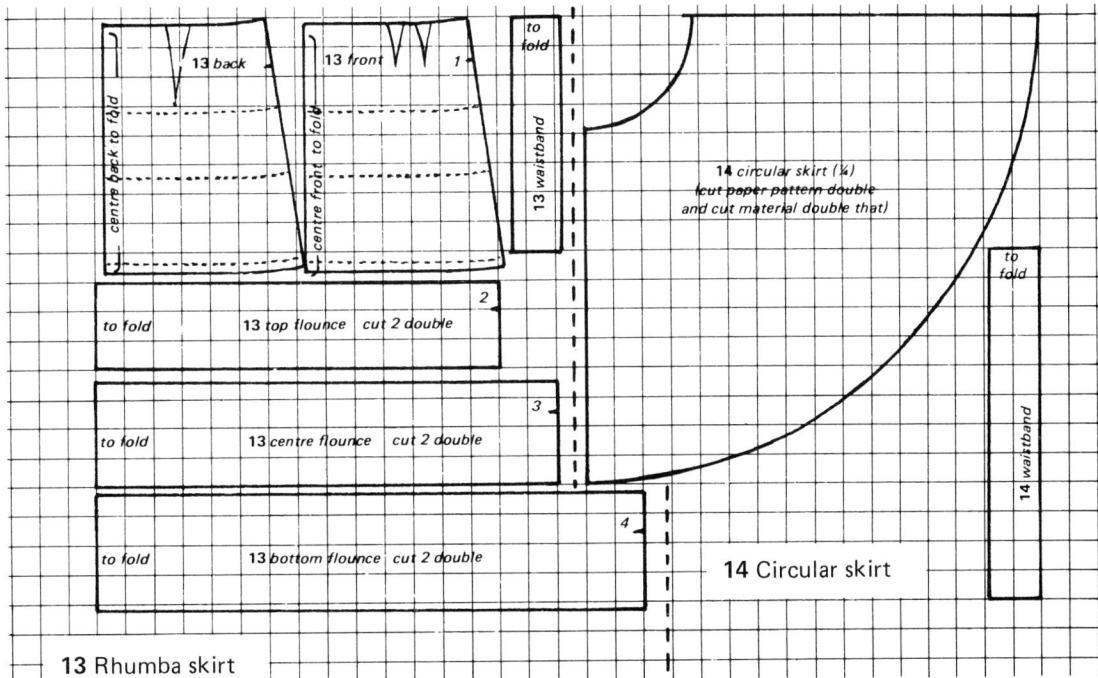

13 back   13 front   1

centre back to fold

centre front to fold

13 waistband

to fold

14 circular skirt (¼)
(cut paper pattern double
and cut material double that)

2

to fold   13 top flounce   cut 2 double

3

to fold   13 centre flounce   cut 2 double

to fold

4

to fold   13 bottom flounce   cut 2 double

14 waistband

14 Circular skirt

13 Rhumba skirt

12 Wrap-over skirt

12   Wrap-over skirt

See p. 32 for pattern pieces. Pin, tack, stitch and press back and front darts. Join back and front pieces together at the sides (notch 1). Press. Turn back and press the facings of both front pieces. Pin or tack for the moment.

Attach the waistband and the strip of Velcro, to hold the 'wrap-over' of the waistband in place to fit the wearer.

Pin up, press and tack the hem. Machine zig-zag the raw edge and slip-stitch in place; oversew the hem edge of the facing invisibly.

If a curved finish to the wrap-over is required, as in the sketch, temporarily pin the facing wrong side out and, using a saucer or round tin or something similar, chalk a line round a quarter of it from the crease of the facing to the crease of the hem. Carefully stitch round this line. Tie off ends of thread. Trim off surplus material. Turn right side out and press the resulting smooth curve. Then slip-stitch hem and facings into position.

13 Rhumba skirt

See p. 33 for pattern pieces. Pin, tack, stitch and press darts in front and back main pieces of skirt. Join front and back main pieces (notch 1) and stitch in a small 11 or 12 cm zip; attach waistband and waist fastener.

Mark position of the top and centre flounces clearly on the main skirt with pins, chalk, pencil or tacking.

Join the side seams of the three flounces (notch 2). Stitch a line of machining round the top edge of each flounce, about 1 cm in, using the longest stitch.

Either bind the bottom edge of each flounce with contrasting bias binding, or turn a very tiny double hem and machine.

Put up the top edge of each flounce as in Hint 10 and 'stroke' gathers evenly.

13 Rhumba skirt

Attach the bottom flounce as in skirt 10, then the centre flounce to the marked position, and finally the top flounce.

14 Circular skirt

See p. 33 for pattern pieces. If your material is wide enough to cut skirt without the need to join skirt pieces, stitch round the waist edge using a

14 Circular skirt

long stitch. If not, join and press the side seams first.

Attach the waistband, pulling up the line of stitching to fit it and enclosing a length of elastic securely joined at the ends inside the waistband. This gives a snug but comfortable fit and takes the weight of the skirt. It also avoids the need for a zip.

Beach wear

Beach or sports wear is very expensive to buy, yet so simple and cheap to make that it seems sensible to try a few adaptable holiday outfits. The pretty, gathered bikini swimsuit is in soft cotton, which gives a bit of extra shape to the still under-developed figure, but also accommodates, because of the fullness, more generous vital statistics! The second bikini is briefer and simpler and was made of stretchy fabric, with ties at the back and neck to allow a comfortable fit for any size.

The shorts are very simple. They can have a waistband, or elasticated waist, pockets at the back, front or both of whatever shape or size you wish – the pockets can also be inserted in the side seam as the zip jacket (see p. 54). Turn-ups are an option, and shorts can be whatever length you wish.

15 Shorts

See p. 36 for pattern pieces. Make whatever patch pockets you have decided on and pin, tack and stitch them into position. (Side seam pockets are also attached to side edges at this stage.)

Join the left and right back and front short inner leg seams, and press (notch 4).

With right sides together match notches 2 and 3. Pin, tack, stitch and press.

Pin side seams and try on; adjust to fit over hips, then stitch and press.

Neaten raw edges of the legs and the waist, then turn up the bottoms of each leg; pin, tack and slip-stitch into place.

Join the ends of a length of wide elastic to fit the waist, and enclose it in the waist hem. Pin, tack and stitch. If a waistband is desired, darts as in the straight skirt (see p. 32) must be put in before pockets are attached; a zip is inserted in the centre front or left side seam, and the waistband is attached instead of the elasticating of the waist.

15 Shorts

35

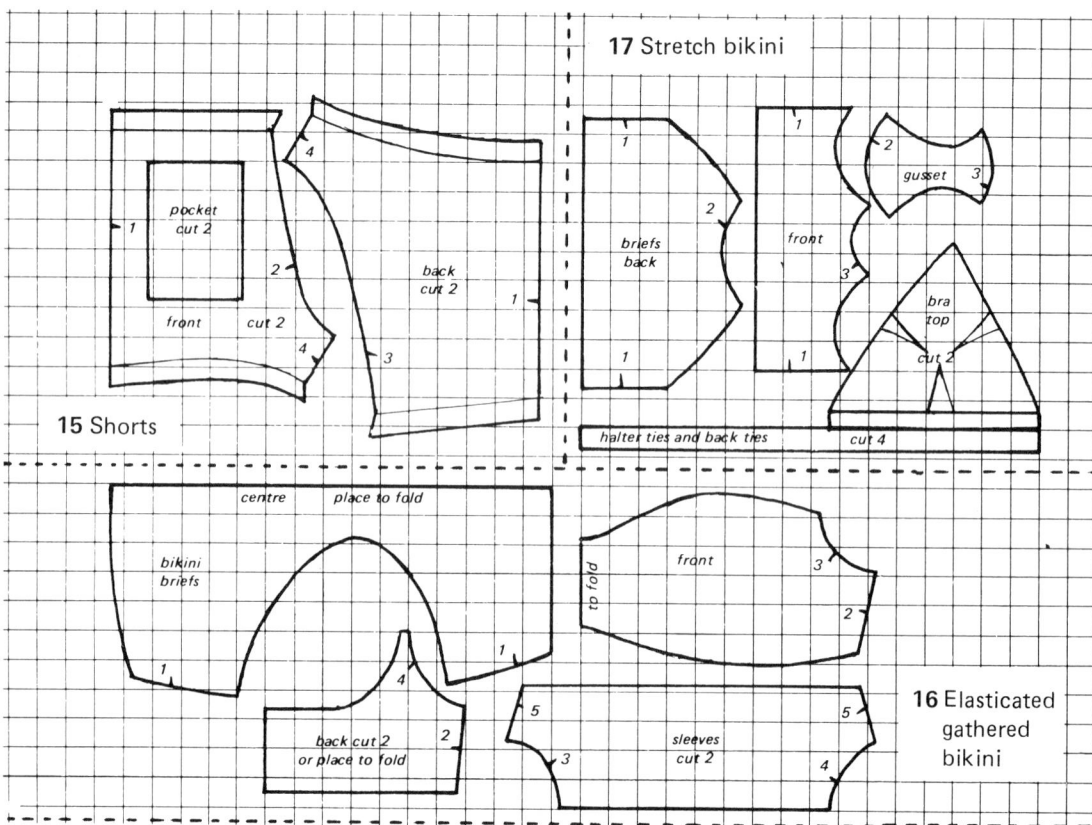

17 Stretch bikini

15 Shorts

pocket cut 2

front cut 2

back cut 2

briefs back

front

gusset

bra top cut 2

halter ties and back ties   cut 4

centre   place to fold

bikini briefs

back cut 2 or place to fold

to fold

front

sleeves cut 2

16 Elasticated gathered bikini

16   Gathered bikini

See p. 36 for pattern pieces. Join left and right sides of the briefs (notch 1) with narrow machine and fell seams. Press.

Turn up the leg edges with bias binding, and turn down a hem round the waist. Thread narrow, strong elastic through leg binding to fit thighs firmly but comfortably, and slightly wider elastic through waist seam to fit.

Join front and back pieces of the bikini top, matching notches 2; use machine and fell seams. Then join the underarm seams of the sleeves matching notches 5.

Join the sleeves to the bodice, matching notches 3 and 4. Press, then neaten the double raw edge to stop fraying.

Turn up and stitch a narrow double hem round the bottom edge of both sleeves and round the bottom edge of the bodice. Turn down the neck edge all round with bias binding.

Thread strong, narrow elastic through sleeve, rib and neck seams or binding, but enlist a friend to help adjust the 'top' comfortably before you finally join the ends of the lengths of elastic.

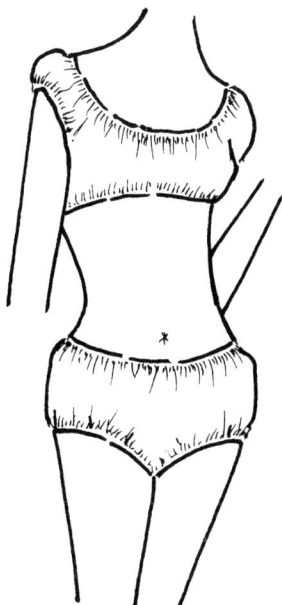

16 Elasticated gathered bikini

17 Stretch bikini

See p. 36 for pattern pieces. Join gusset to back and front of bikini briefs matching notches 2 and 3; use machine and fell seam. Join side seams (notch 1) with machine and fell seams.

Turn down a single hem round waist edge either using a zig-zag stitch over raw edge, or with straight stitching if edge has been neatened, enclosing a length of elastic to fit the waist comfortably.

Turn up a narrow single hem in the same way round each leg, and thread elastic through to fit the thigh comfortably.

Stitch and fasten off securely the three darts shaping each half of the bikini top, and press.

Turn down and stitch (preferably with zig-zag stitch) the four upper edges of the bikini top, or turn down with bias binding.

Overlap the right half of the bikini top over the left half, about 3 cm, and stitch securely along bottom edge.

Turn up the entire bottom edge in the same way as the top edges.

Make four narrow ties about 45 cm long and stitch them very neatly and securely to the two top points and the two outer points of the bikini top to form the halter neck ties and centre back ties. If you feel ties are too fussy, make one long strip for the halter neck, and join the centre back ties with a strong hook and eye, or elasticate the band round the ribs under the bust.

17 Stretch bikini

The styles here are simple, but with distinctly oriental overtones to the pyjamas and short dressing gown. I used a blue patterned trim on white, very light, airy polyester jersey for the pyjamas and on a heavier, non transparent, toning blue polyester jersey for the kimono. The nightdress is a very simple, square-yoked, full-skirted style, in white, light, airy stretch fabric, with nylon lace yoke and narrow lace edging on the skirt hem. The elegant housecoat is double-breasted, closely fitted at the waist, with a swirling seven-panel skirt, big dramatic shawl collar and deep, turn-back cuffs. It was made in white washable non-iron, non-fray, heavy polyester jersey fabric, with scarlet collar, cuffs and pocket facings for dramatic contrast. It was made for summer wear and could have had short, cuffed sleeves instead. Combining plain and patterned fabric is effective, and it looks just as good in a warmer fabric for winter wear, perhaps with matching or contrasting quilted satin or nylon for the collar etc.

18 (a) and (b)   Chinese pyjamas

Trousers

See p. 41 for pattern pieces. Join left front and back trouser pieces at inner leg seam (notch 1). Press flat. Then do the right leg likewise.

With right sides facing, match notches 2 and 3 of each half of trousers, and stitch right round

18(b) Chinese pyjamas

from front waist to back waist, in a machine and fell seam. Press.

With right sides together, stitch both side seams. (If you have chosen style 18(a) leave the bottom 28 cm unstitched.)

Turn down a hem round the waist, enclosing a length of elastic joined securely at the ends to fit the waist comfortably.

For 18(b) turn up bottom edge of each leg to suit. Stitch and press. For 18(a) the facings at the bottom of each leg and around the slit must be attached. Place the *right* side of the bottom leg facing to the *wrong* side of the bottom edge of the pyjama leg. Stitch. Press the facings up on the right side and pin and tack in place. (If the facing fabric is non-fray, no hem is needed.) If it is likely to fray, then a small hem must be turned in and tacked.

Apply the facings to either side of the leg slits in the same way, mitring the corners. Then tack. Stitch the *whole* facing into position with zig-zag stitch over the raw edges, or straight stitch if a hem has been turned. Face the other leg in the same way.

Jacket

For both pyjama jackets, join the shoulder seams of back and front pieces (notch 1) and press.

Join side seams (notch 2) and press. If you are making 18(a) leave bottom 24 cm unstitched.

Join centre front (notch 9), leaving 28 cm unstitched at the top. Press.

Apply the neck-opening facings, and also the two armhole facings (notches 4 and 5) in the same way as for the trouser bottoms and side slits. Press out, pin and tack the facing in position on the right side.

For style 18(b) stitch two or three lines of shirr-elastic round the waist, or apply a casing around inside jacket waist, enclosing a length of elastic, ends joined, to fit your waist comfortably. Then turn up the bottom edge with a small double hem. Press.

For 18(a) apply facings to bottom edge and side splits, as for trouser bottoms.

Stitch both halves of mandarin collar together except at neck edge. Turn right side out and press. Attach collar to neck line, matching notch 8 and mitring the corners. Press. Turn in

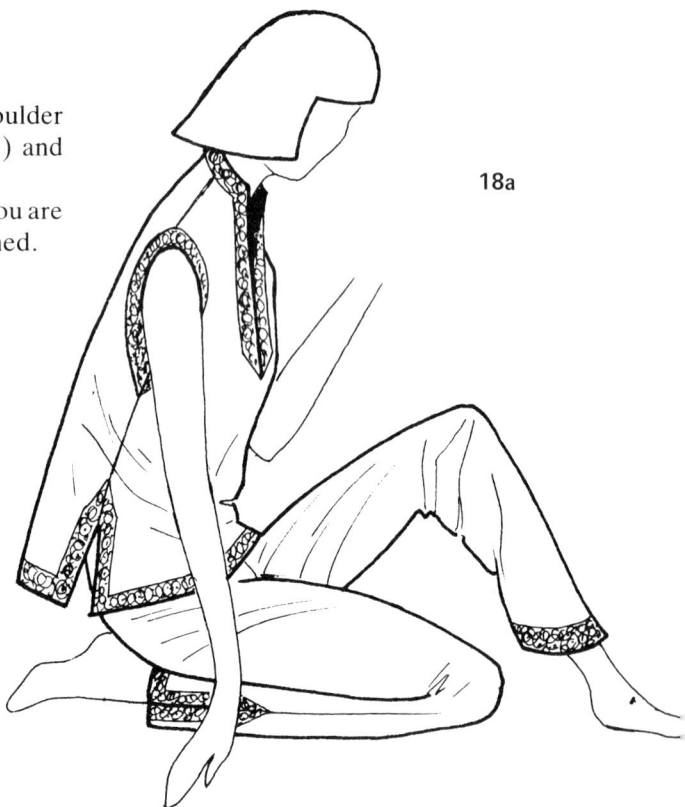

18a

40

18 a and b Chinese pyjamas

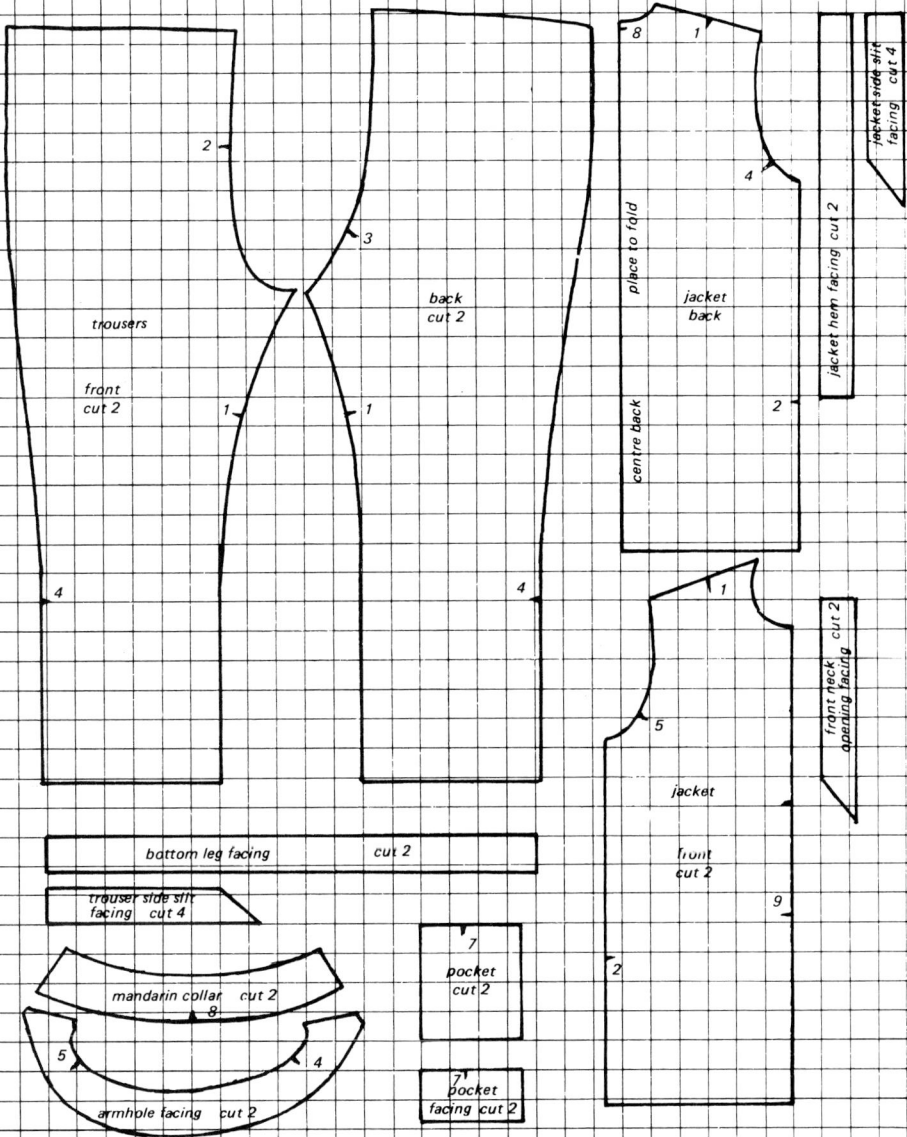

trousers

2

3

back
cut 2

front
cut 2

1

1

1

4

4

place to fold

centre back

8   1

4

jacket
back

2

jacket hem facing cut 2

jacket side slit
facing   cut 4

1

5

jacket

front
cut 2

9

2

front neck
opening facing   cut 2

bottom leg facing   cut 2

trouser side slit
facing   cut 4

mandarin collar   cut 2
8

5   4

armhole facing   cut 2

7

pocket
cut 2

7
pocket
facing cut 2

41

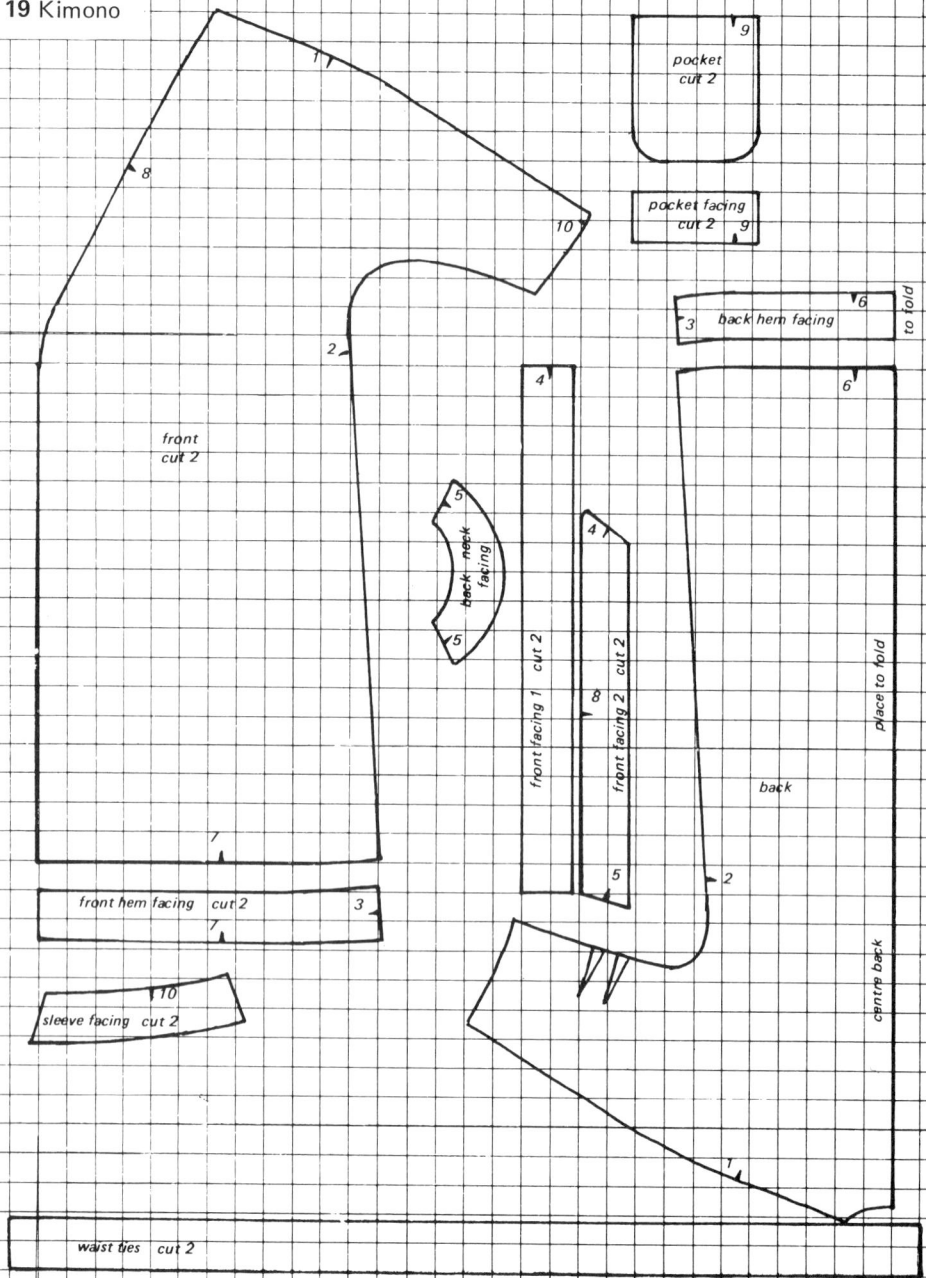

19 Kimono

pocket
cut 2

pocket facing
cut 2

back hem facing

front
cut 2

back-neck
facing

front facing 1   cut 2

front facing 2   cut 2

place to fold

to fold

back

centre back

front hem facing   cut 2

sleeve facing   cut 2

waist ties   cut 2

20 Housecoat

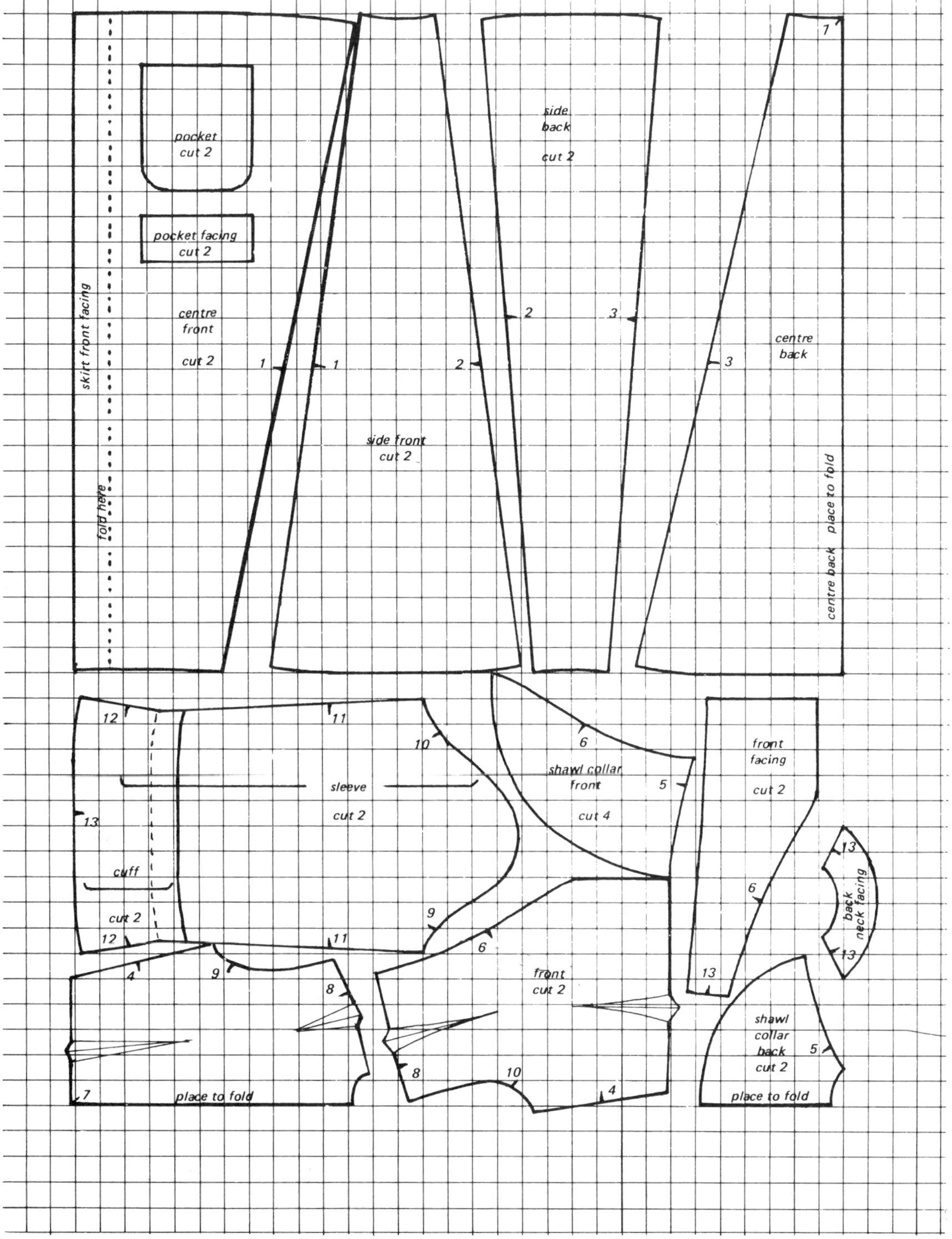

pocket
cut 2

pocket facing
cut 2

skirt front facing

centre
front

cut 2

fold here

1   1

2

side front
cut 2

side
back

cut 2

2

3

2

3

centre
back

centre back   place to fold

7

12   11

10

6

13

sleeve

cut 2

shawl collar
front

cut 4

5

front
facing

cut 2

13

cuff

cut 2

12

11

9

6

back neck facing

13

4   9

8

front
cut 2

6

6

13

7   place to fold

8   10

4

shawl
collar
back
cut 2

5

place to fold

43

the bottom edge of inner collar and pin, tack
and hand-hem it to the pyjama top neck. Press.
Zig-zag the right side hem to match the other
facings.

Make pockets, matching notch 7 of pocket
and facing. Press single hem round pockets, pin
in position and stitch down. Press.

19   Kimono

See p. 42 for pattern pieces. Stitch the two
elbow darts in the sleeves of the back piece and
press.

With right sides together, pin, tack, stitch and
press the shoulder seams and upper arm seams,
matching notches 1 of the left and right fronts
and the back piece.

Join the underarm and side seams of back and
fronts, matching notches 2. Press. Leave 5 cm
unsewn at waist of right side seam. Reinforce
opening with zig-zag stitching.

Join short length of facing material to ends of
each waist tie. Join the edges, press open seams,
stitch across one end, pull inside-out and re-
press the finished ties. Pin to the waist positions
of each front, wrong side of ties to wrong side of
fronts, open end to front edge, in line with each
other.

Join the three pieces of the bottom hem
facing, matching notches 3. Press. Then,
matching notches 6 and 7 to bottom hem, right
side to wrong side of hem, attach as in pyjamas.

Join the two front facing pieces for left and
right fronts, matching notches 4; then, matching
notches 5, pin facings to the back neck facing.
Stitch and press. Attach entire facing to fronts
and neck edges of the kimono, as before,
mitring the bottom corners as in the pyjamas.
The waist ties are secured in the process.

Join the ends of the bottom sleeve facings
(notch 3), and press. Apply the facings to
bottom of sleeves as before, matching notch 10.

Apply the pocket facings (notch 9). Turn in a
small hem around raw edges, pin in position and
stitch carefully. Tie off ends securely.

19 Kimono

20 Housecoat

See p. 43 for pattern pieces. Pin, tack and stitch centre front panels to side front panels (notch 1), and centre back panel to side back panels (notch 3). Press seams and front facing.

Join side seams (notch 2). Press. Try on and pin first to get close-fitting waist.

Pin, tack, stitch and press front and back bodice darts and the four shoulder darts. Press flat. Join shoulder seams (notch 8) with darts meeting. Press flat. Try on and then join side seams with a close-fitting waist (notch 4). Press flat.

With right sides together, join back under-collar to front under-collar pieces (notch 5). Press seams open. With right sides facing, match completed under-collar to the bodice at shoulder, centre back and notches 6. Press flat, clipping curves where necessary.

Join the three upper-collar pieces in the same way. Join the back neck facing and the two front facings (notch 8). Press. With right sides together, join completed upper-collar to the completed facings, matching notches 6, shoulder seams, etc. Press flat, clip curves where necessary.

With right sides facing, join completed upper-collar and facings to completed under-collar and bodice, matching seams, etc. Turn right side out, pulling collar edge carefully into shape. Press. Tack the edges of the facings into position.

With right sides together, join cuff facings to bottom edges of sleeves. Adjust to longest stitch and machine round upper curve of each sleeve about 1 cm in. With right sides together, join sleeve edges, matching notches 11 and 12, and cuff seam. Press open. Turn up cuff facings. Pin tack and stitch edge into place. (Zig-zag stitch over the raw edges is neater and flatter.) Turn back cuff to suit your arm length and press.

Try on bodice to make sure waist is a close fit, underarm fit is loose and comfortable, and shoulder seams are right length for your shoulders. Pin in each sleeve, matching notches 9 and 10 and underarm seams, to the armholes. Gently pull bobbin thread of the stitching round

20 Housecoat

top sleeve curve, to ease surplus material into the armhole. Tack, stitch and press.

Check exact waist position on bodice and mark clearly with pins or chalk. With right sides facing, pin bodice to skirt, around waist mark, matching seams, darts, centre front, centre back, side seams and facing edges. Stitch, and press seam upwards. Top-stitch this seam in place on the right side to give a ridged waistline. Turn back facings again and tack in position.

Stand on a table wearing slippers and get a helpful friend to pin up the bottom hem to clear the ground. Take off and lay out on a table; smooth out the curves of the hem and re-pin. Cut off surplus material, leaving a good centimetre for the hem. Stitch over raw edge with zig-zag stitch, or top-stitch.

Either slip-stitch the previously tacked facings into permanent position or, better still, zig-zag very carefully with a small stitch round the entire inner edge of the facings. (This is much better if the housecoat will be washed.) Oversew the bottom of the facings and the skirt together by hand.

Mark the position of the four buttonholes to fit your bust and waist, and work by hand or machine very carefully. Mark button positions through buttonholes and sew buttons on securely.

Face pockets. Turn in hem round other edges. Pin in place and stitch down carefully. Secure ends. Press.

21 Nightdress

See p. 47 for pattern pieces. Join centre back and centre front seams (notch 2), then side seams, matching notch 3. Use machine and fell seams. Press. Stitch round the upper edge of skirt, 1 cm in, with longest stitch (Hint 10).

Join back and front yokes, both inner and outer lace ones, at the sides, matching notch 1. Press flat.

Place the two yokes together, with right sides facing, and carefully stitch all round the neck edge, across shoulders and round armholes.

21 Nightdress

46

21 Nightdress

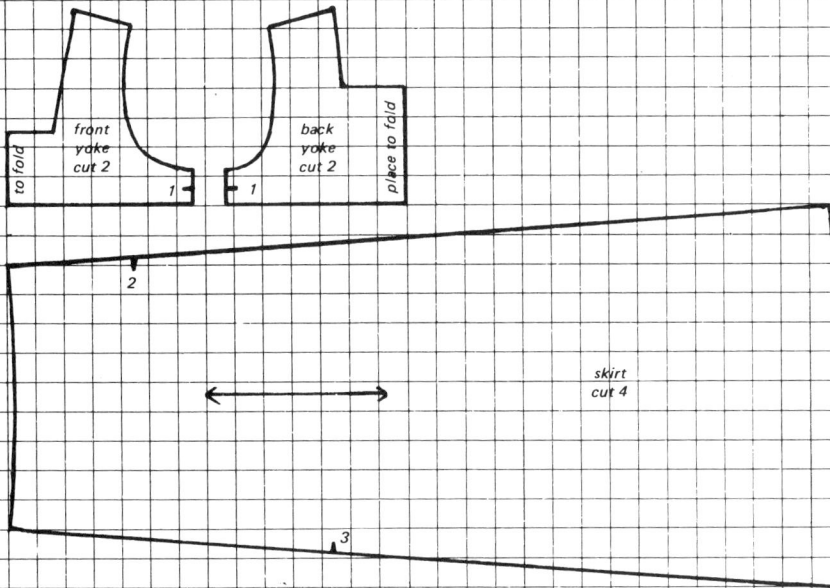

Pattern labels: to fold · front yoke cut 2 · 1 · 1 · back yoke cut 2 · place to fold · 2 · skirt cut 4 · 3

Clip curves and turn right sides out. Pull seam edges to shape and press.

Gently pull the bobbin thread of the long-stitch machining round top of skirt from both ends, to approximately the same length as the yoke bottom edge. Match side seams, centre front and back of skirt and outer yoke, and pin. Ease material into gathers as evenly as possibly between these points and pin, tack carefully and stitch. Press seam upwards. Turn garment inside-out, turn up bottom edge of yoke lining and pin the lining exactly and neatly over the gathered seam. Hand-hem securely into place, using the backs of the machine-stitching instead of the fabric.

Place the front and back shoulder seams together (edges butting) and oversew with neat, close stitches, securing well at each end. Press the oversewn edges flat.

Turn up a small hem round bottom of nightdress. Press. Pin, tack and stitch a narrow lace edging to bottom of the hem.

Jackets and waistcoats

Jackets is a rather misleading word for this collection of garments, designed to be worn over a blouse or jumper in most cases. Bolero 22 was made in the same velvet as the four-gored skirt (pattern 9 on p. 30) to be worn over the silk shirt blouse (pattern 6 on p. 26) making a very elegant outfit – or, of course, over the other open or buttoned-up-neck shirt blouse (patterns 4 and 5 on p. 23-5). Gilet 23, with the back gathered into a belt at the waist, was made of the same fabric as the wrap-over games skirt (pattern 12 on p. 33), but it can be worn over any skirt or slacks and does not need to match either. The other gilet (pattern 24) was made as an alternative to the safari jacket, over the safari-suit trousers and shirts; the overblouse (pattern 25) and waist coat (pattern 26) were made of denim to wear with jeans and shirts, but again these tops can match or contrast with whatever you wish. Pullover 27 of a brown, tweed-effect, polyester jersey was made to wear with a straight skirt (pattern 8 on p. 29) with or without a shirt or jumper. The casual jacket (pattern 28) with stand-up collar, zip front, elasticated cuffs and bottom, and side-seam pockets, was made in showerproof, polyester gaberdine in a stone shade with a scarlet lining, but it also could be made in a lightly quilted, showerproof fabric that is popular and quite cheap. The hooded jacket (pattern 29) was made in a heavy, knobbly, green-orange-fawn tweed. We lined it with green and it was a warm and practical winter outfit, with dark green or brown trousers, or straight skirt, and a shirt, pullover or jersey picking up one of the colours in the tweed.

22 Bolero

See p. 50 for pattern pieces. Pin, tack and stitch the bust darts in the two bolero front pieces, and the waist darts in front and back pieces. Press flat.

With right sides together, match notches 1 and 2. Pin, tack, stitch and press seams open. Neaten raw edges if necessary.

Match notch 7, with right sides of back neck facing and bolero front facings together. Stitch and press. Match shoulder seams and notch 6 of bolero and facing, with right sides together. Pin,

22 Bolero

49

22 Bolero **23** Gilet (1) **24** Gilet (2) **25** Overblouse **26** Waistcoat

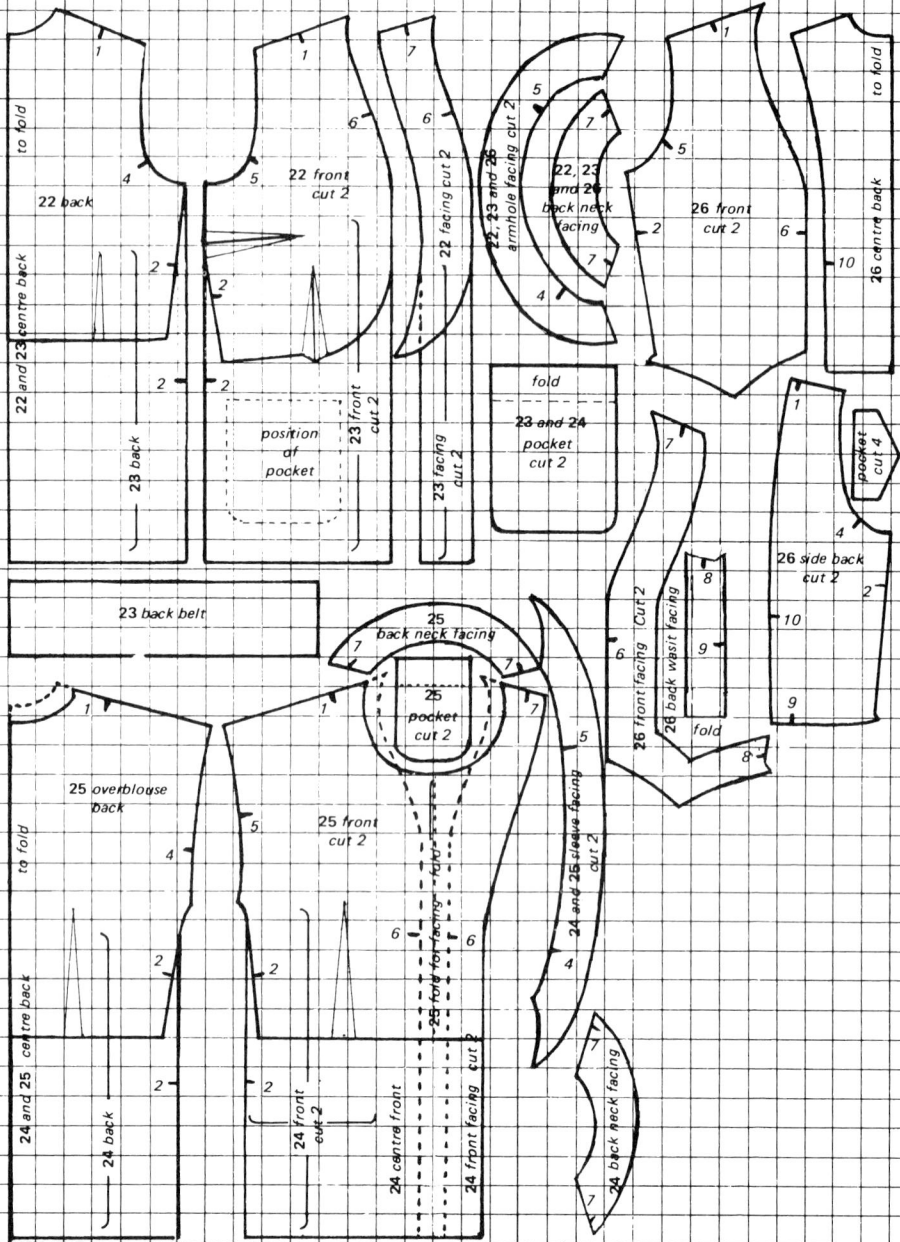

to fold

22 back

22 and 23 centre back

4

5

1

1

22 front
cut 2

2

2

2

2

23 back

position
of
pocket

23 front
cut 2

7

6

1

6

22 facing cut 2

23 facing
cut 2

22, 23 and 26
armhole facing cut 2

5

7

5

2

4

22, 23
and 26
back neck
facing

7

fold

23 and 24
pocket
cut 2

7

1

6

10

26 front
cut 2

26 centre back

to fold

1

pocket
cut 4

4

2

26 side back
cut 2

10

9

fold

8

23 back belt

25
back neck facing

7

25
pocket
cut 2

7

26 front facing Cut 2

26 back waist facing

8

9

6

25 overblouse
back

to fold

24 and 25 centre back

1

1

5

4

25 front
cut 2

2

2

2

2

24 back

24 front
cut 2

6

6

25 fold for facing fold

24 centre front

24 front facing cut 2

24 and 25 sleeve facing cut 2

5

4

24 back neck facing

7

7

50

tack and stitch. Clip all curves, turn right side out and press.

Join underarm seam of both armhole facings and press. With right sides together, match notches 4 and 5 of bolero and armhole facings. Stitch, turn right side out and press.

Neaten edges of all facings, if necessary.

Turn up bottom edge with matching bias binding, in line with the end of facings, and invisibly hand-hem the binding in position. Catch down the facing underarm and on shoulder seams enough to hold the facing in place, or, if you prefer, slip-stitch them in position all the way round.

Top-stitch round armholes and entire bolero about 5 mm in from the edge. Fasten off neatly and press.

23 Gilet (1)

See p. 50 for pattern pieces. With right sides together, match shoulder notches 1 and side-seam notches 2 of back and two front pieces. Stitch and press flat. Neaten raw edges if necessary.

Make facings for neck and front and armholes, and stitch and press exactly as in the bolero instructions (*see above*).

Turn up a hem at the bottom to suit yourself, and slip-hem it into position. Cut off surplus facing, turn in a small hem and oversew neatly to main fronts in accurate line with the hem. Press.

If you decide to have pockets, make them, at this stage. Position them and stitch carefully into place. Tie ends securely. Press. Top-stitch armholes, neck and front edges as for bolero (*see above*).

Join long edges of half belt. Press flat. Stitch one end to give an arrowhead finish. Trim off surplus. Turn inside-out, press, and turn in the other end to match. Oversew with very small close stitches. Press. Top stitch all round.

Machine two lines of long stitches across back at waist level and draw up carefully, or use shirr-elastic, or stitch a length of ordinary elastic

23 Gilet (1)

24 Gilet (2)

inside gilet at the waist to reduce the material to fit. Position the belt over the gathered waist, as in the illustration, and attach it permanently with two buttons.

It is, of course, just as fashionable without the belt and gathers, and left loose.

24 Gilet (2)

See p. 50 for pattern pieces. With right sides together, join shoulder and side seams matching notches 1 and 2. Press flat, clipping curves underarm.

Join facings for fronts, back neck and armholes, as for gilet (1), match them to notches 4, 5, 6 and shoulder or underarm seams, as before. Stitch, clip all curves, turn, press and neaten as for bolero or gilet (1).

Make and position pockets if they are desired, as above. Top-stitch and press as above.

25 Overblouse

See p. 50 for pattern pieces. Stitch and press waist darts in back and both front pieces. Match notches 1 and 2 and stitch shoulder and side seams. Clip curves, press flat.

Join facing (notch 1) to back neck facing (notch 1). Press flat. With right sides together,

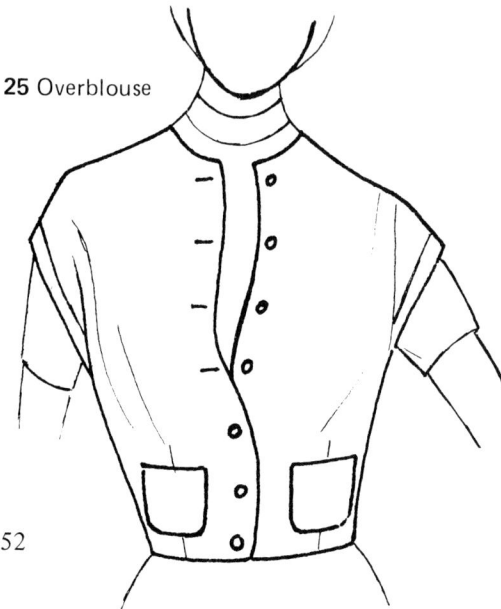

25 Overblouse

match facing neck to overblouse neck. Stitch round accurately 1 cm in. Clip curves. Turn right side out and press down neck and front edges. If material is flimsy, before stitching and turning, iron on to the facing fronts, a lightweight Vilene interlining to take the strain of buttons and buttonholes.

Make and apply sleeve facing as in gilet (2), and turn up bottom edge (waist) as in bolero instructions.

Mark positions of buttons and buttonholes, and complete these neatly. Alternatively, apply studs or 'ginger snaps'.

26 Waistcoat

26 Waistcoat

See p. 50 for pattern pieces. Match notch 6 on centre back and each side back piece. Stitch, press double, and top-stitch. This completes the waistcoat back.

Follow the instructions for the bolero, remembering to join the back waist facing piece to the front facings (notch 3), instead of having to turn up the bottom with bias binding.

Make the two imitation pockets. Turn right side out and top-stitch round them, before positioning them and stitching into place.

27 Pullover

If these three facings are self colour, to lie inside the garment, position them right sides facing. If they are contrasting, and meant to be outside the pullover, place the right side of the facing to the wrong side of the garment. Stitch, matching seams carefully. Turn right side out (or in), after clipping all curves, and press.

For inside facings, neaten edges and top-stitch as in bolero; for outside facings, turn carefully a small hem around each facing edge, tack and top-stitch down very neatly. Fasten off carefully and press. Ordinary edge top-stitching can be done if you wish. The pullover will probably be more fashionable if the facings are all top-stitched boldly at both edges, but be accurate! Chalk a line on the outside and follow it carefully.

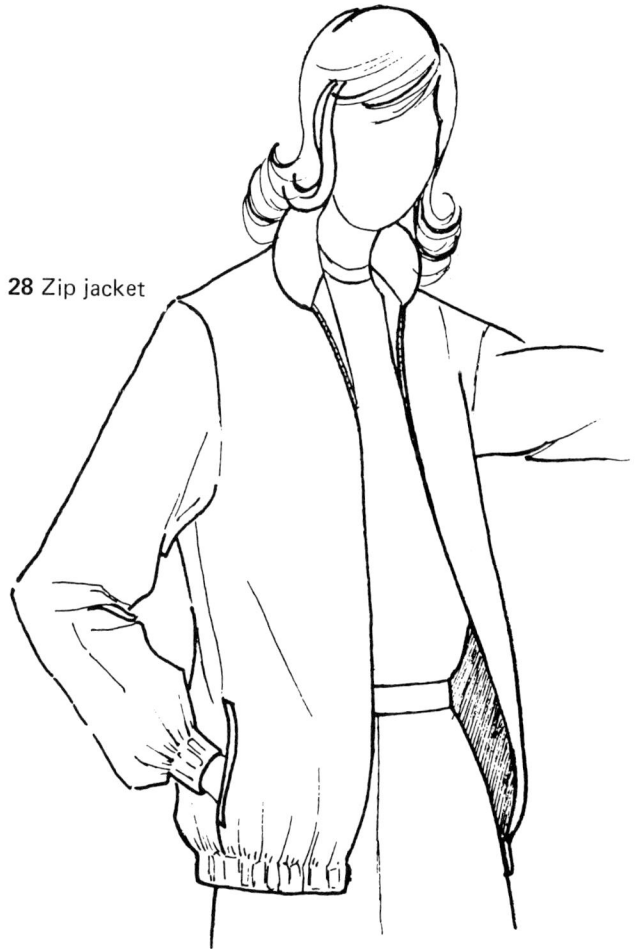

28 Zip jacket

27 Pullover

See p. 54 for pattern pieces. Matching notches 1 and 2, join back and front pieces and press seams flat. Neaten if necessary.

Stitch and press flat elbow darts in both sleeves. Match notch 3 and join sleeve edges. Press flat.

Check that armholes are comfortable. Run line of long stitching round top of each sleeve. With right sides together, match carefully underarm seams and notches 4 and 5 of sleeves and pullover body, easing surplus material of sleeve tops into armholes by gently pulling bobbin thread of long stitching. Tack, stitch and press well. Try on for sleeve length and bodice length. Cut off surplus, less 1 cm.

With right sides facing, join notches 7 and 9 for neck facing. Press seams flat. Join ends of sleeve and bodice bottom facings and press flat.

28 Zip jacket

See p. 54 for pattern pieces. Join the four pocket pieces (exactly matching each other) to the side seams of back and front pieces. Press joins flat *in line*.

With right sides facing, match notches 2, and stitch down to, then round the pocket, then down to the bottom of the side seam. Nick the side seams above and below the pockets so that they lie flat against the jacket fronts. Press the rest of the side seams flat. Stitch a short line of machining across the flat seam to hold the pockets in place and reinforce the spot that takes a lot of strain.

Join shoulder seams (notch 1) and front facings (notch 6) enclosing one half of an open-ended zip fastener in each side. Press right side out, to the inside of the jacket front, which brings the teeth of the zip to the outer edge of each front. Tack securely and top-stitch.

Make and insert the sleeves as instructed for the pullover. Turn up the bottom edge of each sleeve, enclosing a length of wide elastic to fit loosely round the wrists. Stitch securely.

Attach back neck facing to front facings, matching notches 7. Press flat, and pin to main garment. With right sides together, join front and back collar. If material is soft, use an iron-on interlining on inner collar, to give a little 'body' and enable it to stand up if it is required to do so. Matching notch 8 and centre front, tack collar into position, right side of outer collar to right side of jacket. Stitch, clip and press up. Turn in inner collar edge over neck seam, and hem very neatly into position.

Note Take care to position the two halves of the zip fastener together exactly opposite each other, before positioning the two ends of the collar

Note If a lining is wanted, it is cut from the same pattern as the jacket, less the facings and the depth of the hems at the wrist and bottom. It is made as a 'second jacket', with the facings, and stitched to the elasticated hems.

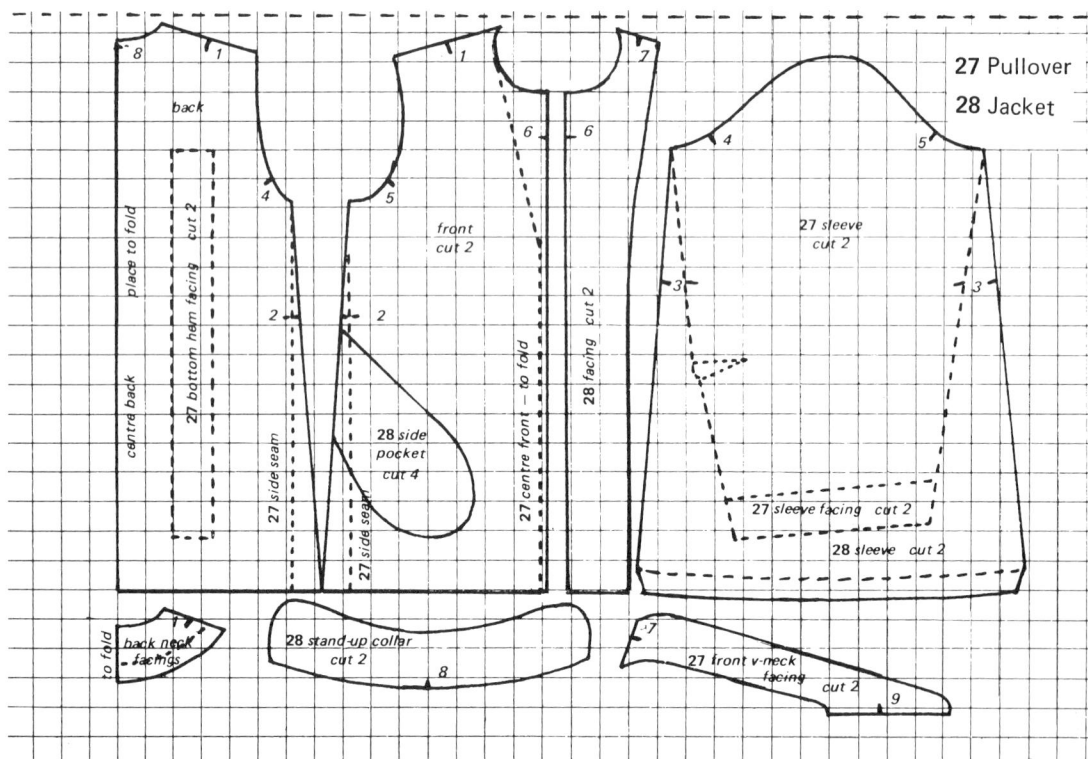

29 Hooded belted jacket

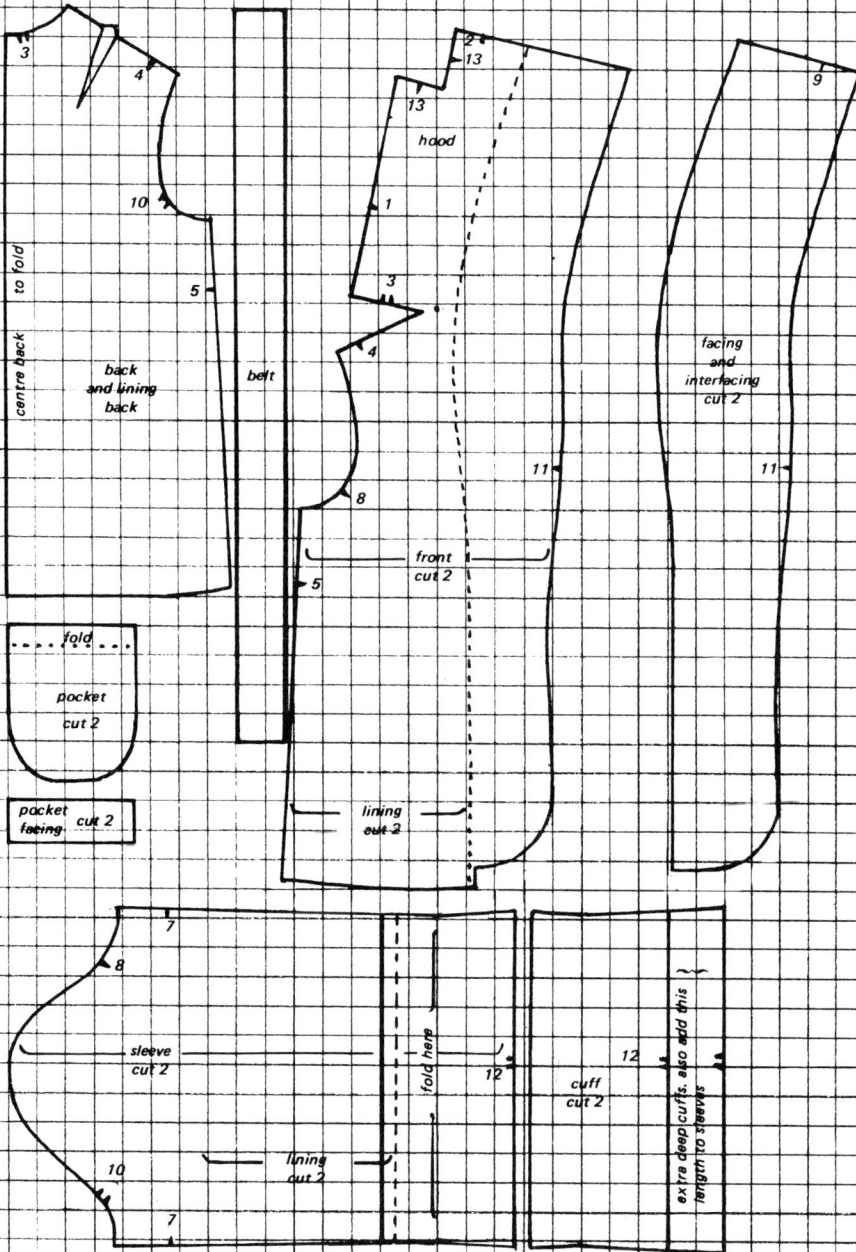

centre back · to fold

3

4

10

5

back
and lining
back

belt

pocket
cut 2

pocket
facing · cut 2

2
13

13

hood

1

3

4

8

front
cut 2

5

lining
cut 2

11

9

facing
and
interfacing
cut 2

11

7

8

sleeve
cut 2

10

7

lining
cut 2

fold here

12

12

12

cuff
cut 2

extra deep cuffs, also add this
length to sleeves

fold

29 Hooded, belted jacket

See p. 55 for pattern pieces. Stitch and press back shoulder seam darts.

With right sides together at all times, match notch 4, and stitch to dot, to join the shoulder seams. Nick front/hood carefully to that dot. Press seam open flat.

Join side seams (notch 5). Press open.

Join centre top hood seam (notch 2) and centre back hood seam (notch 1). Press seams open.

Matching notch 3, join neck edge of jacket to neck edge of hood. Clip curves. Press open flat.

Match centre top hood seam to centre back hood seam, and notch 13, stitch and press.

Make up the lining exactly as the jacket above, and after joining the two jacket facings, matching notch 9 and pressing the seam flat, join the lining to the completed facing.

Matching notch 7, join sleeve edges. Press seams flat. Join sleeve cuffs to sleeve linings, and join sleeve lining edges matching notch 7. Press seams flat. Stitch a line of long-stitch machining round top curve of both sleeves and linings. Matching left sleeve and armhole at notches 10 and 8 and underarm seam, and easing surplus material into armhole by gently pulling up long-stitch bobbin thread till it fits, pin securely, tack, stitch and press. Put in the other sleeve. Join linings and cuff bottoms to sleeve bottoms. Press.

Attach pocket facings to pockets, press down and slip-stitch in position. Turn in and tack a small hem round each pocket. Press, then position on jacket, and stitch carefully round, close to the edge. Fasten off securely.

You now have virtually two jackets. With right sides together, match seams and notch 11. Tack and stitch facings and hood edges together. Turn right sides out and press. Ease up and pin sleeve lining tops into armholes of lining. Slip-stitch in place. Turn up hem round bottom to line up with facing seams. Slip-stitch in place. (If material is soft, iron on a strip of interlining to the hem, to give 'body' before stitching.) Turn up lining hem, clear of the bottom, and stitch in place. Press. Make belt, and attach buckle. It may be helpful to make belt stays on both side seams to hold the belt if you often leave your coat open and the belt unbuckled.

Top-stitch all the edges 1 cm in, and press the cuffs up to suit your arm length.

29 Hooded belted jacket

Trousers and trouser suits

This small group of garments seemed very popular. The safari suit was made in heavy cotton with metal buttons and buckle; the light stone colour looked very military, very smart, and yet very casual. It could, of course, have long sleeves, as in the tunic which we made as an alternative top over the trousers. The number of pockets the tunic has is optional and the neck can be varied. The low belt is narrow and loosely tied, or even a cord or rouleau could look effective. The width of the pants in all the garments is a matter of choice. The 'boiler-suit', reminiscent of American Army 'fatigues' was made in denim with zip front, gathered waist, and pointed yokes, collar and cuffs and large patch pockets. The dungarees in heavy red polyester jersey had an elasticated waist, small bib and wide braces with metal buckles and looked very dashing over any of the shirts already made or any pullover.

30 Safari suit

See p. 59 for pattern pieces.

Trousers

Stitch and press the waist darts in front and back of each trouser piece. Match notch 10 of front and back of left and then right leg. Stitch and press open. With right sides together, match notches 11 and 12, and stitch right round from centre front waist to centre back. Clip curves and iron flat. If zip is to be put in centre front, unpick amount needed. Tie ends securely and pin, tack and stitch in zip.

Try on the trousers inside-out. Pin up the sides and legs to fit snugly. Take off, lay flat and chalk a stitching line, smoothly, about 1-2 cm outside the pins, to allow for movement. Tack, stitch and press open flat. If you prefer your zip in the side seam, unpick the necessary length of the top left side seam and insert the zip.

Stiffen the waistband piece, if necessary, and attach it to the trousers, after checking and trimming the waistline. A gathering line can be machined to ease trousers top into waistband, if necessary (Hint 10). Stitch on waist fastener securely to fit.

Wearing shoes, pin up the bottom of each leg to the required length. Better still, get a friend to do it. Slip-stitch or herringbone-stitch the hems in place after trimming.

Note If fabric needs to have edges neatened, try to do it after trying on and trimming off any surplus, and before you stitch and press seams. (Hint 9).

Jacket

Matching notch 8, join front yokes to jacket fronts, and back yoke to jacket back. Press seams upwards. Top-stitch.

Matching notch 7, join front facings to front jacket. Press and tack down to hold. Join shoulders, matching notch 1, and side seams, matching notch 2. Press open.

32 Boiler Suit

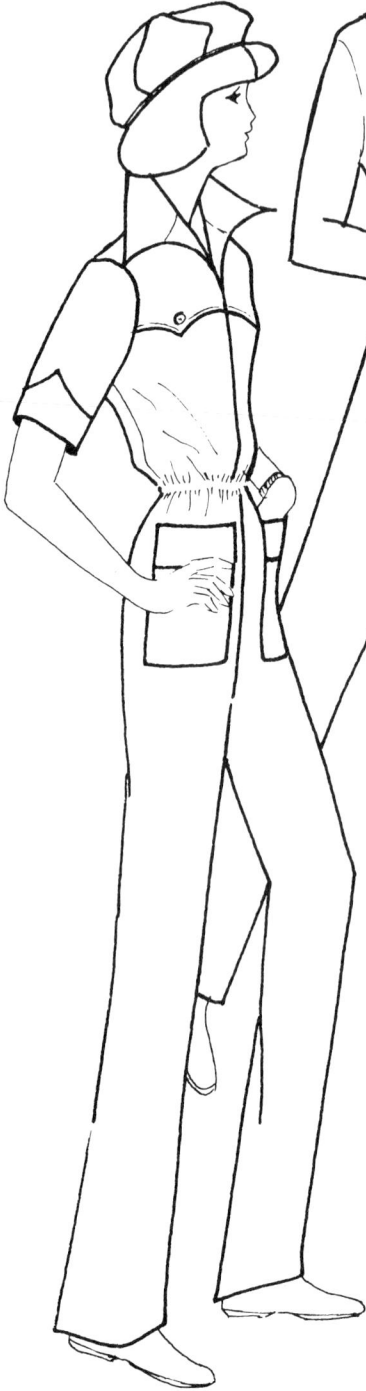

33 Dungarees

30 Safari suit

31 Tunic top

30 Safari suit

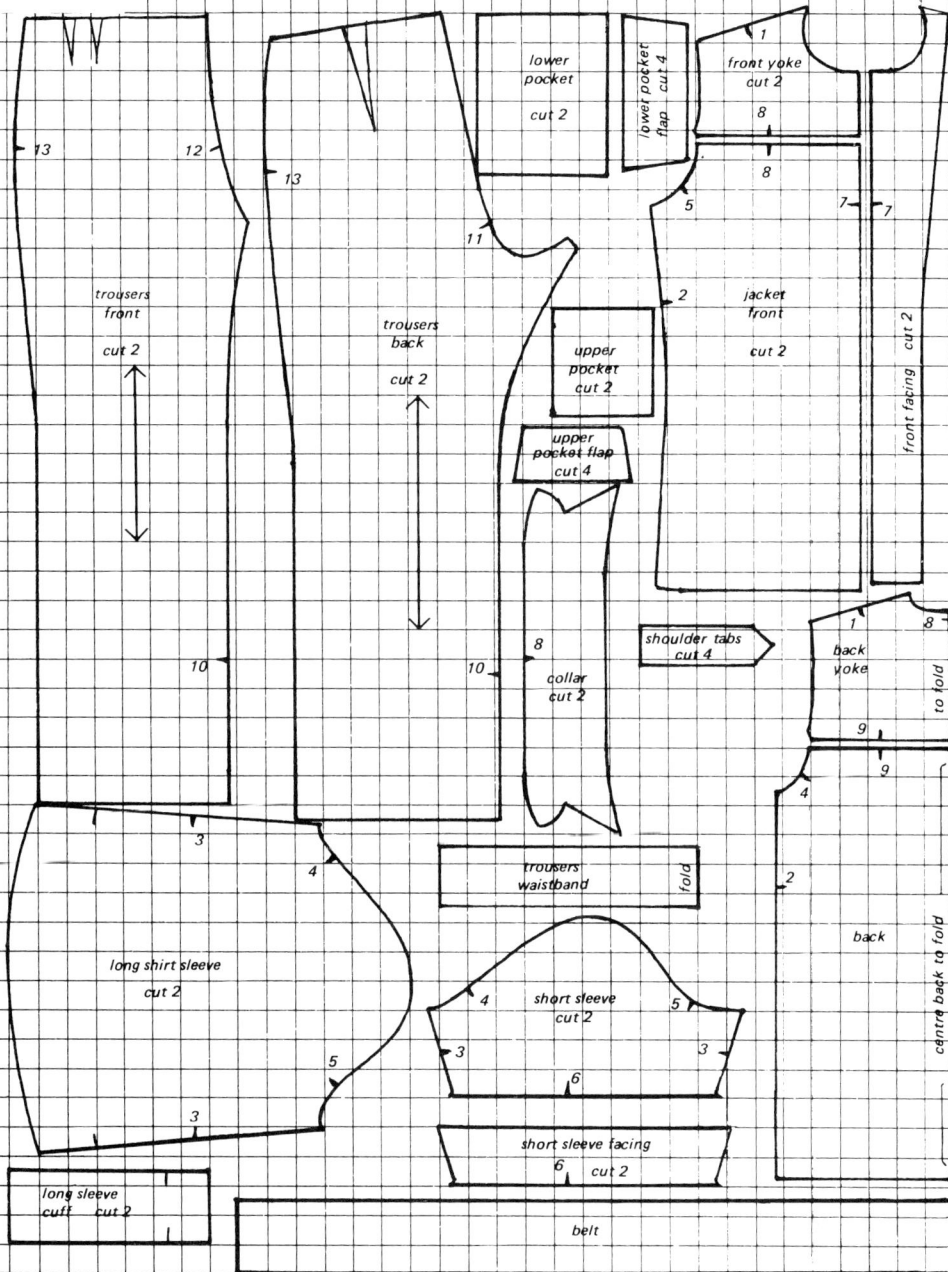

trousers
front

cut 2

13

12

13

trousers
back

cut 2

11

lower
pocket

cut 2

lower pocket
flap cut 4

front yoke
cut 2

1

8

8

5

7 7

2

jacket
front

cut 2

front facing cut 2

upper
pocket
cut 2

upper
pocket flap
cut 4

shoulder tabs
cut 4

back
yoke

1

8

to fold

9

9

4

10

10

8

collar
cut 2

2

back

centre back to fold

3

4

trousers
waistband

fold

long shirt sleeve

cut 2

4

short sleeve
cut 2

5

3

3

5

6

3

short sleeve facing

6 cut 2

long sleeve
cuff cut 2

belt

59

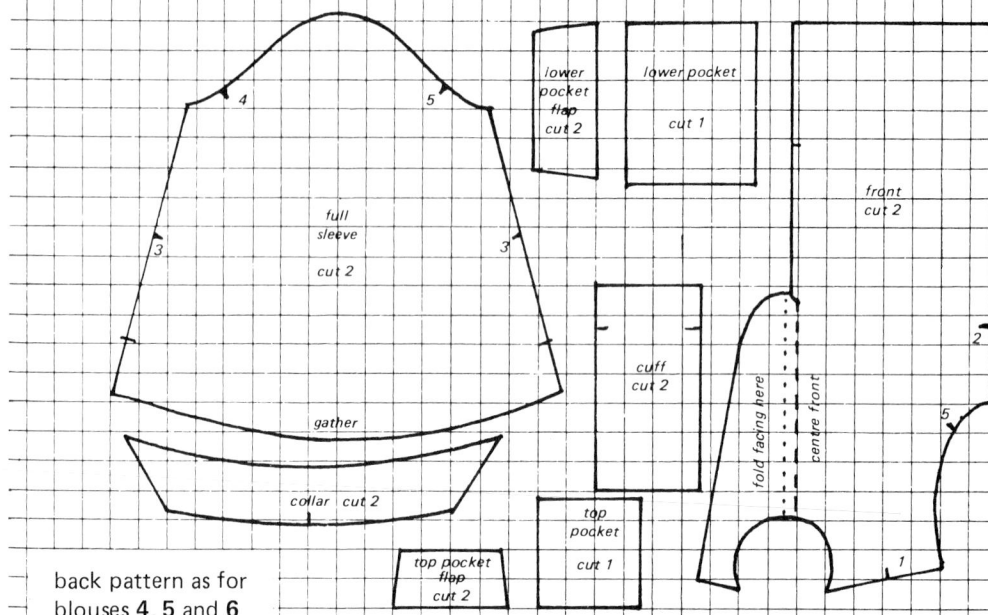

31 Tunic top

lower pocket flap cut 2

lower pocket cut 1

front cut 2

4

5

full sleeve cut 2

3

3

cuff cut 2

fold facing here

centre front

2

5

gather

collar cut 2

top pocket cut 1

back pattern as for blouses **4, 5** and **6**

top pocket flap cut 2

1

Turn down and stitch top hem on all pockets. Press a small hem all round the other sides. Make the four pocket flaps and the shoulder tabs, placing pieces right sides together, stitching round three edges, turning right side out, pressing and top-stitching. Make the buttonholes in the flaps. Pin the shoulder tabs in place, and position the pockets to suit. Place the flaps above the pockets, right side to right side of jacket. Stitch pockets carefully in place, and stitch across the open end of the flap about 1 cm above top edge of pocket. Press flap downwards over pockets and stitch across double thickness of flap to hold it down. Fasten all ends securely.

Make up short sleeves and set them in, as instructed in shirt blouse 4 (*see p. 25*), or long sleeves if desired, as instructed in blouse 7 (*see p. 26*).

Attach collar, as instructed in blouse 4.

Make belt, and belt stays. Try on and pin two stays in place on side seams and stitch. Stitch on buckle and pierce holes.

Mark button and buttonhole positions, down front and on flaps and cuffs. Work buttonholes and stitch on buttons, not forgetting two for the shoulder tabs.

31 Tunic top

See p. 60 for pattern pieces. The tunic is made up exactly the same way as blouse 5 (*see p. 25*) for the neckline, and blouse 7 (*see p. 26*) for the sleeves. The pockets illustrated are from the safari jacket.

The only variation from the instruction already given in these projects is that the centre seam is stitched up to the facing, as marked, and a *careful* nick is made to the marks, so that the facings can be pressed back and turned in at the bottom and stitched, before the blouse 5 instructions etc. are carried out.

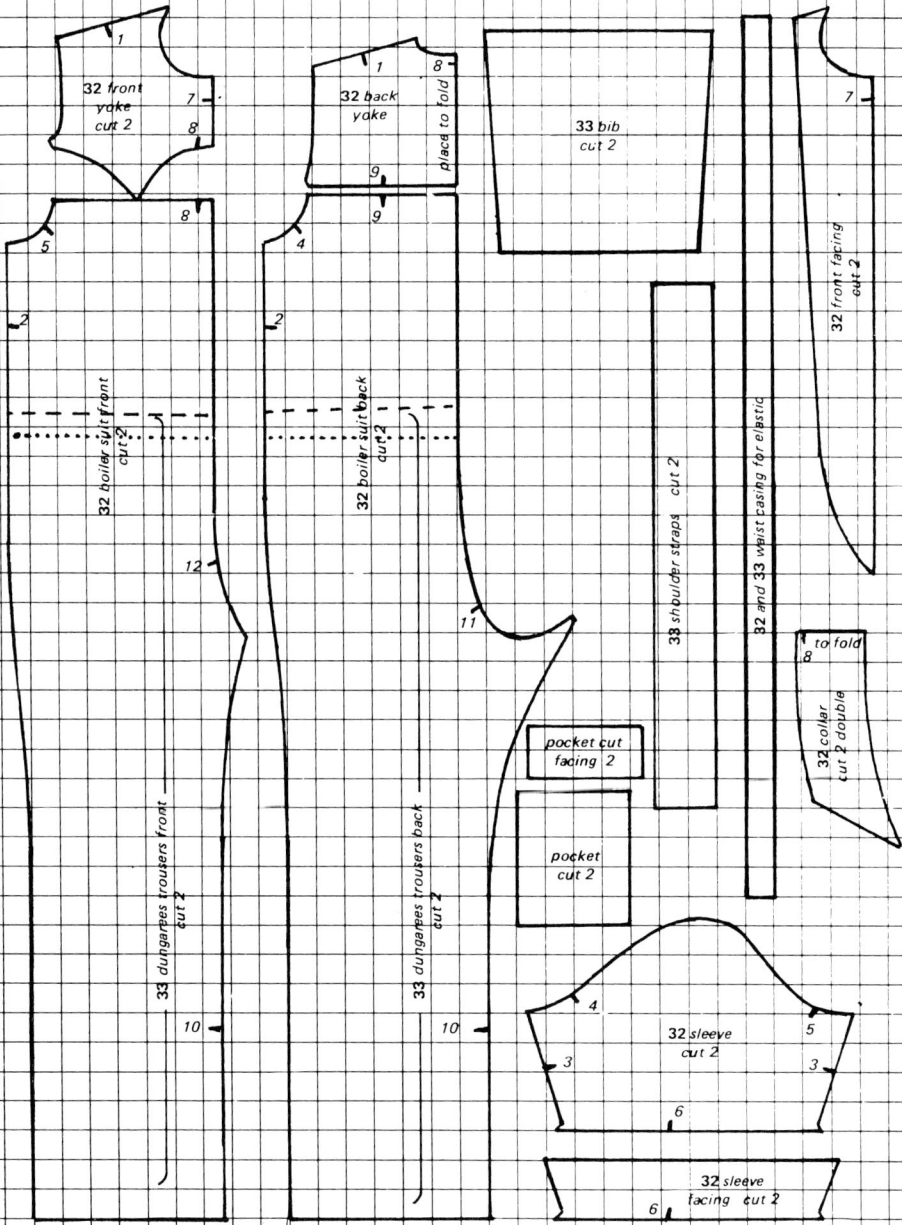

32 front
yoke
cut 2

32 back
yoke

place to fold

33 bib
cut 2

32 front facing
cut 2

32 boiler suit front
cut 2

32 boiler suit back
cut 2

33 shoulder straps   cut 2

32 and 33 waist casing for elastic

to fold

32 collar
cut 2 double

33 dungarees trousers front
cut 2

33 dungarees trousers back
cut 2

pocket cut
facing 2

pocket
cut 2

32 sleeve
cut 2

32 sleeve
facing cut 2

32 Boiler suit

See p. 61 for pattern pieces. Matching notch 8, stitch turned-in pointed edge of yoke to each front, close to the edge. Stitch another line about 7 mm in. Matching notches 10, join the back and front inner leg seams. Press flat.

With right sides together, join both halves from notch 12 round crutch to notch 11 and up the centre back. Clip at curves and press open flat.

Matching notch 9, attach back yoke in the same way as the fronts.

With right sides facing, and with half the closed-ended zip placed carefully between garment and facing, tack securely. Be sure that each half of the zip matches the position of the other exactly before stitching. Turn to right side, press and tack in position. Join shoulder seams. Press.

Make the collar and turn right side out. Press and attach to the neckline. Press. Top-stitch a double row of stitching round zip and collar.

Make sleeves and pockets with outside facings as instructed in blouse 4 (*see p. 25*) and housecoat 20 (*see p. 45*). Position pockets at hip level and stitch double rows of top-stitching round edges. With boiler suit turned inside out, try on, and get a friend to pin up both side seams from ankle to armhole, retaining fullness at waist. Tie a piece of elastic or string round the waist and let it find its natural, comfortable position. Mark this line clearly with chalk or pins. Take off garment carefully. Stitch up side seams and press them flat.

Pin and tack the strip of waist casing to the inside waist of the boiler suit – its centre over the chalked line – from front facing edge to front facing. Stitch neatly. Thread a length of wide elastic through the casing to draw up the waist to a snug fit, and stitch both ends very securely just under the front facings. The elasticated waist allows the wearer to bend without difficulty.

Put in the sleeves, as instructed in blouse 4 (*see p. 25*) and press. Turn up the bottom of the legs, as instructed for the safari suit (*see p. 57*).

Note Remember that all the facings and the yoke can be straight or pointed, as you wish.

33 Dungarees

See p. 61 for pattern pieces. Join inner leg seams of front and back, left and right legs, (notch 10). Press. Match notches 11 and 12 and, with right sides facing, stitch round and clip at curve. Press open flat. Try on, pin up both side seams. Chalk in a stitching line (Hint 5). Stitch, press open. Turn down and pin a hem at the waist, to enclose waist-fitting length of wide elastic, (see instructions for elasticated waist, p. 30). Press.

With right sides together, stitch round bib all except about 8 cm at the bottom. Pull inside out. Press. Neatly close the 8 cm gap with small oversewing stitch.

Place the middle of the bib bottom against the folded edge of the centre front. Oversew the whole bottom edge to the waist fold or zig-zag the two edges together. Press flat.

Make the pockets and the shoulder straps. Position the pockets and stitch in place. Enclose the elastic in the waist hem and stitch it down. Pin the shoulder straps to the waist hem, either side of centre back. Cross them, bring ends over the shoulders and fasten to the front top corners of the bib, with buttons and buttonholes, buckles, studs, or whatever you choose.

Turn up both leg bottom hems as in the safari suit (*see p. 57*).

Hats

The hats in this collection are made from all kinds of oddments of material. The 'pull-on' cap and the hood were of light, fairly bulky, stretchy fabrics; the safari hat matched the safari suit, and the others were of various woollen mixtures and velvets.

34 Pull-on hat

See p. 65 for pattern pieces. Join two of the crown pieces, and then the other two. Press the seams open flat, clipping if necessary. Join the two halves together. Clip and press.

Make the lining in the same way. Place the lining inside the crown and pin together round bottom edge.

Join the two short ends of the brim. Press flat. Right sides together pin and tack one long edge of the brim to the bottom edge of the crown. Stitch, and press brim downward. Turn a small hem on the other long edge and fold brim over to bring hem (or brim edge if material does not fray) up to first seam. Slip stitch the brim into position and press. Turn up the brim to suit you.

35 Peaked caps (a) and (b)

See p. 65 for pattern pieces. Join the six pieces of the crown, three and three, and press seams open, as for pull-on hat (see above). For (b) join the centre back seam and press flat.

With right sides together, and a piece of

34 Pull-on hat

stiffening of a fairly heavy weight on top, stitch round the curve of the brim. Layer the seam. turn right side out. Press well. Top-stitch round the brim curve, at 1 cm intervals.

Make the crown lining exactly as the crown itself and pin inside round brim edge. With a strong thread, gather the brim edge to fit your head comfortably and fairly loosely. For style (b) also gather the top edge of the crown with strong thread and pull up as tight as possible before fastening off securely. Spread all the gathers evenly around.

Pin the brim to the crown at centre front, and

stitch right across the brim and then back. Bind over the whole gathered brim edge, with the headband, right sides facing, and starting at centre back. Turn over, leaving about 1 cm showing outside and a wider band inside to fit the head. Top-stitch band outside. Cover a flat button with cloth and stitch over the centre top join, or stitch a circle of fabric over it.

35 Peaked cap

36 Fur-trimmed hood

36 Fur-trimmed hood

Note 1 Real fur, even if it is only rabbit, looks best, but imitation fur does very well. Fur framing the face is very flattering.

Note 2 Fit the hood *frequently* while pinning, sewing and pressing the darts, to get a well-shaped and loosely fitted crown.

36   Fur-trimmed hood

See p. 65 for pattern pieces. Pin, tack and stitch slightly curved darts in both front and back pieces. Press. Pin front half of hood to back half, and try on to see if more darts are needed to shape it loosely to the head. Then, with right sides together, stitch both halves together, matching the darts. Clip and press. Top-stitch.

Join centre front under chin seam, clip, press and top-stitch.

Join the ends of the fur facings by hand so that they lie flat. Try to match the way the fur lies. Turn *out* a small hem round the face and bottom edge of the hood and attach the fur facings to the hems and at the inner edge using small hand-hemming stitch.

37   Safari hat

See p. 65 for pattern pieces. Join the four pieces of the crown and make the lining as for pull-on cap (*see p. 63*).

Join centre back seam of inner and outer hat brim. Press and, with right sides together, join them and stiffener interlining round brim edge. Layer seam edge. Turn right sides out. Press. Top stitch at 1 cm intervals round whole brim. Clip around inner edge.

Fit brim inner edge to be overlapped by bottom edge of crown and lining. Tack and neatly zig-zag stitch all round. Top-stitch on the outside, or zig-zag stitch, to hold the loose edge neatly on the inside. If you wish, put in a ribbon headband, and an outer hat band for decorative purposes.

Note The pattern allows for a wide or a narrow brim.

34 Pull-on hat   **35** Peaked cap   **36** Fur-trimmed hood   **37** Safari hat   **38** Beret   **39** 'Spanish' hat

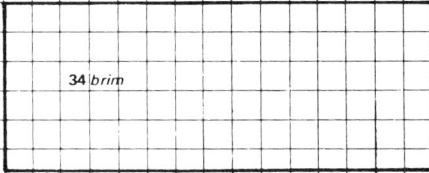

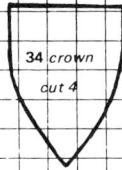

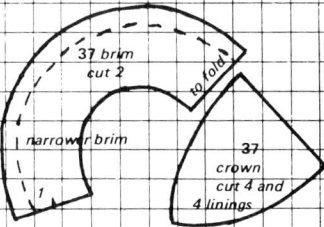

34 brim

34 crown
cut 4

37 brim
cut 2

to fold

narrower brim

37
crown
cut 4 and
4 linings

If a fuller, gathered crown
is wanted, use this pattern
instead and if a 4-part or
2-colour crown is wanted,
cut here and add 1 cm
seam to each edge.

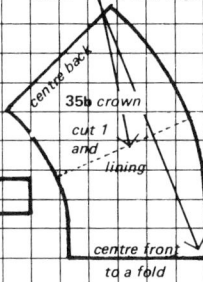

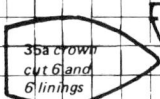

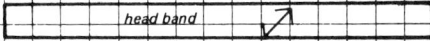

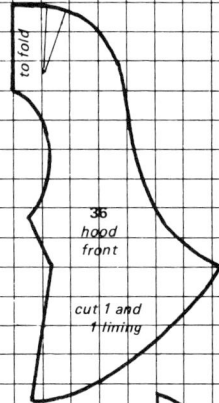

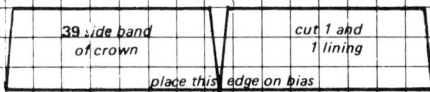

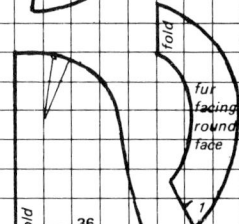

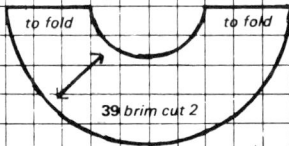

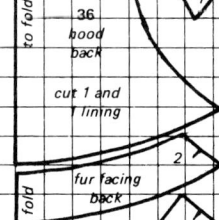

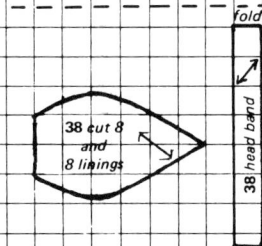

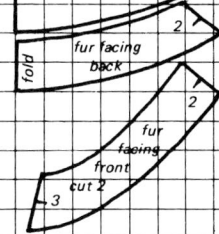

to fold

36
hood
front

cut 1 and
1 lining

centre back

35a crown
cut 6 and
6 linings

35 peak brim
cut 2

35b crown
cut 1
and
lining

head band

fold

centre front
to a fold

fur
facing
round
face

39 side band
of crown

cut 1 and
1 lining

place this edge on bias

to fold

to fold

39 top
crown
cut 1
and
1 lining

to fold

36
hood
back

cut 1 and
1 lining

39 brim cut 2

fold

fur facing
back

fur
facing
front
cut 2

fold

38 cut 8
and
8 linings

38 head band

65

38 Beret

See p. 65 for pattern pieces. Join the crown pieces together in pairs, then halves, then the whole, pressing and clipping seams as they are sewn. Try on. The beret should fit the head comfortably. If it is too loose stitch a line of long-stitch machining and gently pull up to fit (Hint 10).

Bind the head edge in the same way as for peaked cap (*see p. 64*), with 1 cm of headband outside, the rest inside, and a line of top-stitching to hold it in place.

Put on a centre top button as on the peak caps.

Note If a lining is wanted, make it in the same way as the main beret and put it inside before adding the headband.

39 Spanish hat

See p. 65 for pattern pieces. Join left and right side seams of the crown side-band, and press flat. Join the crown top of the hat to the crown side-band, easing one gently to meet the other. Clip and press.

Make the lining in the same way, and pin it inside the crown.

With right sides together, stitch inner and outer brim and a stiff interlining together round outer edge. Layer the seam. Turn right sides out. Press.

Join brim to crown as per instructions for safari hat (*see p. 64*).

Stitch a hat band round to cover the join, or tie a chiffon scarf round it. Pull two lengths of cord or rouleaux, knotted at the ends, through brim just in front of the ears and knot casually under the chin.

38 Beret

37 Safari hat

39 'Spanish' hat

Dresses

Although the illustrations show dresses with full, gathered skirts, remember that they could have unpressed pleats, or the straight, or four-gored skirts, or any of the short skirts, except the wrap-over style, in any length you like, instead. Alternatively, the full, gathered skirt could have any of the blouse styles for the bodices, if you want to ring the changes.

Style 40(a) was made in a navy, red and white soft cotton border print; style 40(b) in an open-weave, white polyester mixture jersey, bound with yellow, and the gathered-to-fit bodice; style 40(c) in a forget-me-not blue silk, which came from a damaged roll on a market stall and so was at a knock-down price.

40   Sun or party dresses

See p. 68 for pattern pieces.

Styles (a) and (b)

Join the skirt panels, matching notches 1 all round. Press open. Leave one seam unsewn for about 15 cm at the top. This is the centre back.

Stitch a line of long-stitch machining round waist edge and pull up (Hint 10) to fit your waist. (Use the strongest possible bobbin thread. We used a fine crochet cotton, which is very strong and unbreakable.) Secure ends temporarily.

Stitch and press the waist and bust darts in front and back bodice pieces, and in the linings, if your material needs a lining to give the bodice stability. Join side seams matching notches 2. Press flat.

If you are making style (a), make the four narrow shoulder ties (flat, or as rouleaux) and pin one to each shoulder point between the right sides, placed together, of the bodice and lining. Stitch round from right centre back, via neck, shoulder, armholes, and so on, to left centre back. Turn right side out and press. This brings shoulder ties to the outside. Tack round to hold in position temporarily.

If you are making style (b), the instructions are the same as for (a) but there are no shoulder ties. Instead the two shoulder edges on left and right, are 'butted' together, and oversewn very neatly and pressed flat; or zig-zigged together. Alternatively, place the bodice and lining (or facings) *wrong* sides together after having joined and pressed flat the shoulder seams, and tack or pin all round. Leave temporarily.

Spread the skirt gathers evenly. Match the side seams, centre front and back, etc., to the bodice, with right sides together. Tack and stitch carefully. Press seam upwards. Pin, tack and stitch zip in place, from centre back (lowest point of V back) down to end of unstitched part of centre back skirt seam. Press. Turn in centre back lining edges, and stitch by hand to the back of the zip stitching, then turn up waist edge of lining and stitch over the gathering to the back of machining. Press. Top-stitch to give a slightly raised waist seam.

40a, b and c Sun and party dresses

N.B. Use the dotted lines on the patterns if you have narrower material or a limited amount. It still gives a very full skirt.

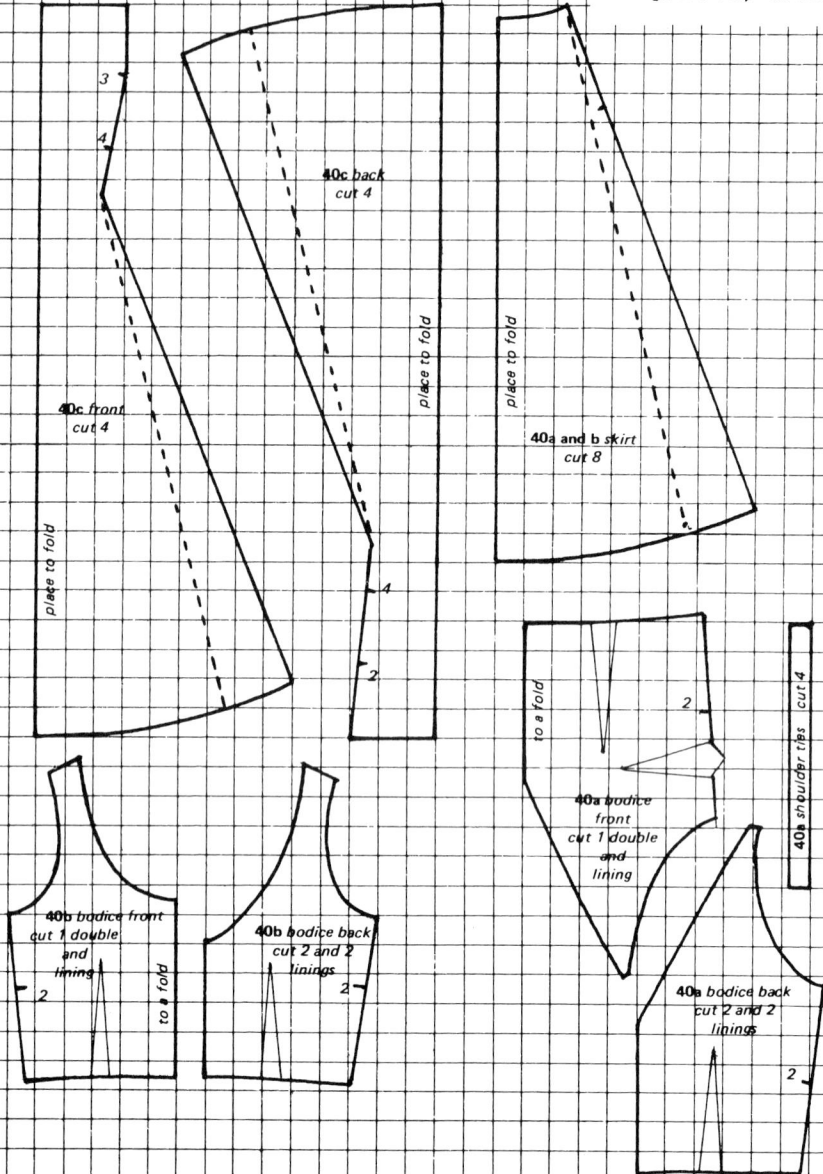

3

4

40c back
cut 4

place to fold

place to fold

40c front
cut 4

40a and b skirt
cut 8

place to fold

4

2

to a fold

2

40a shoulder ribs cut 4

40a bodice front
cut 1 double
and
lining

40b bodice front
cut 1 double
and
lining

2

to a fold

40b bodice back
cut 2 and 2
linings

2

40a bodice back
cut 2 and 2
linings

2

(a)

Returning to the alternative instructions for the style (b) bodice, now that the zip has been stitched in, you can bind the neck and armholes with contrasting bias binding. Another alternative, if your material is stiff enough to need no lining at all, is to turn in the neck and armhole edges with bias binding in place of lining or facings, which, incidentally, would have to be cut from the bodice patterns. Of all the alternatives I recommend a thin lining.

Style (c)

Skirt and bodice sections are cut all in one in this style, so join the eight panels, first the four fronts then the four backs, then the whole back to the front, trimming the two side front bodice edges to match the two side back ones. Press all seams flat. Open centre back seam to about 15 cm below waist, and pin, tack and stitch in the zip fastener.

40 Sun and party dresses

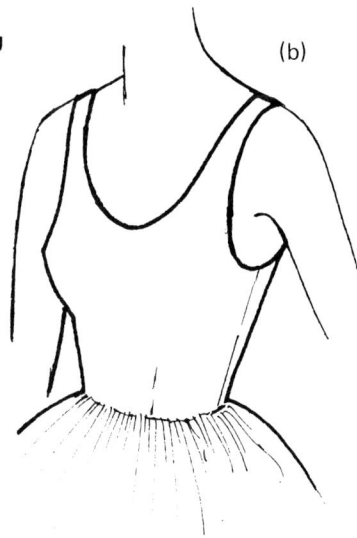

(b)

Neaten all round top edge with zig-zag stitch if possible. Turn down a 2 cm hem and tack. Starting 1 cm from top edge, mark a guideline all round with tailor's chalk or very light pencil dots or lines. Repeat, 5 mm below, then 2.5 cm below that. Repeat every 5 mm and 2.5 cm for approx 32 cm. Using the longest stitch, machine along these lines. If your machine has the attachment with a bar for measuring the distance between lines of stitching, this is much quicker and more accurate. Use very strong thread in the bobbin. (I used fine crochet cotton.)

Pull up the bobbin thread from each end to fit approximately. Make the two very narrow 'shoelace' shoulder straps, or use narrow velvet ribbon.

Try on inside out. Pin shoulder straps roughly into position. Close the zip, then pull up the gathers with the strong bobbin thread (Hint 10) to fit *you* perfectly (wear a well fitting bra when you do this). Tie each end off very securely and snip short as the fitting is done, until the last lines are completed. Carefully 'stroke' the gathers all round to spread them evenly. Adjust the position and length of shoulder straps and stitch in place securely.

Turn up a small double hem round the skirt bottom and machine round. Press.

(c)

Shawls and capes

Two simple patterns for useful over-garments. The shawl would be ideal over one of the party dresses shown in the last chapter to give extra warmth on a chilly summer's evening. It was made from a square piece of very wide, knitted Acrilan in an open, lacy pattern. The fringe was a lucky dip from a market-stall – useful because 15 cm fringing can be expensive to buy in the shops.

Capes always have a slightly dramatic air. They are very easy to make, practical to wear, and whether you favour the short, swinging style with the rather military air, or the longer knee-warming, elegant length, you will be sure to turn more than a few heads. Of course, you could make a really stunning entrance in a floor length cape, if you have a really grand dinner date or dance to dress up for.

The pattern here is simple to cut and make; it has a choice of short or knee lengths; a collar which will stand up or lie flat, and a hood. It has a zip front and arm slits.

It could be dressed up with fur edging, or military braid, or frog or tab fastenings instead of the zip, and so on. If an ankle-length version is required, the pattern pieces just need to be lengthened the necessary amount. If buttons and buttonholes are preferred, the addition of 4-5 cm to the centre front edge of the pattern will give the necessary wrap-over.

41 Evening shawl

Square up, cutting along a thread if necessary. Take off the corners making a gentle curve instead.

Tack the fringe to the edge overlapping the edge about 7-8 mm. On the right side, zig-zag edge of fringe to the fabric. Turn over to wrong

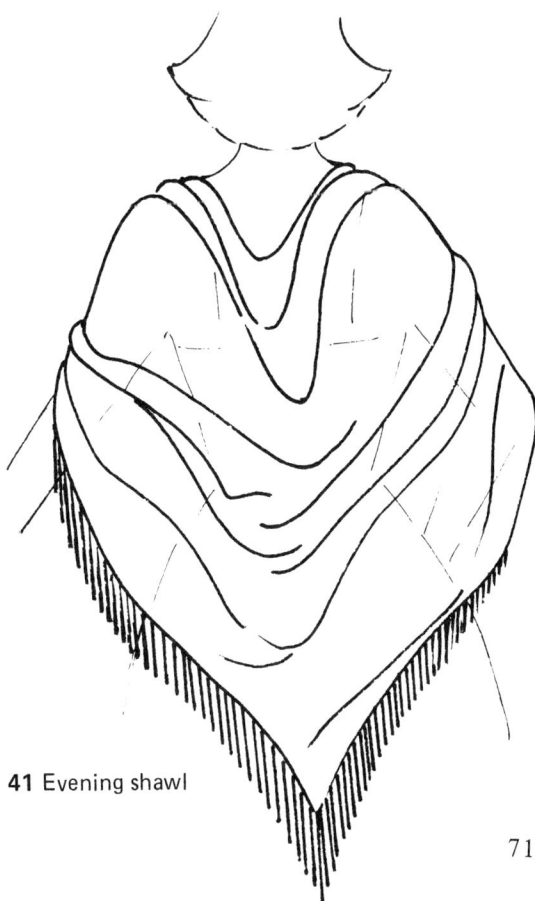

41 Evening shawl

71

side and zig-zag edge of fabric to the fringe. These two lines of stitching make it very secure and fray-proof.

Join the fringe by overlapping for 2 or 3 cm and oversewing together at convenient places in the design.

42 Cape

See p. 73 for pattern pieces. Join the two shoulder seams in the side pieces matching notches 1. Clip carefully, and press to get the curved shoulder line.

Match notches 3 and 4 of the side back and back pieces. Stitch and press seams open. Stitch and press darts to fit shoulder back.

Match notches 2 of side front and front pieces. Stitch and press seam open.

Carefully unpick the pressed down flat seam between the arm slit markings, tying off seam securely at the top and bottom of the openings.

Stiffen slightly the two front facings and the under-collar, by pressing on a medium-weight, iron-on interlining (i.e. Vilene).

Match notches 5 on under-collar with notches 5 on either side front. Stitch and press seam open.

Match notches 7 of back neck facing and front neck facings and join. Press seams open.

Make up the lining and front facings *exactly* as the outer cape was made, including the arm slits.

Match the made-up neck facing to the lining and front facing, either to the top of the lining, *or*, if you used the 'lining cutting lines' marked − − − on the pattern, to the neck edge of the lining. Stitch. Press. Which ever way you choose, the inner and outer cape should be identical.

Attach the upper-collar to the neck facing edge as for the under-collar above.

*If you opted for the hood, match notches 8 of centre back of hood, stitch and press open. then match notches 9 and stitch across top back

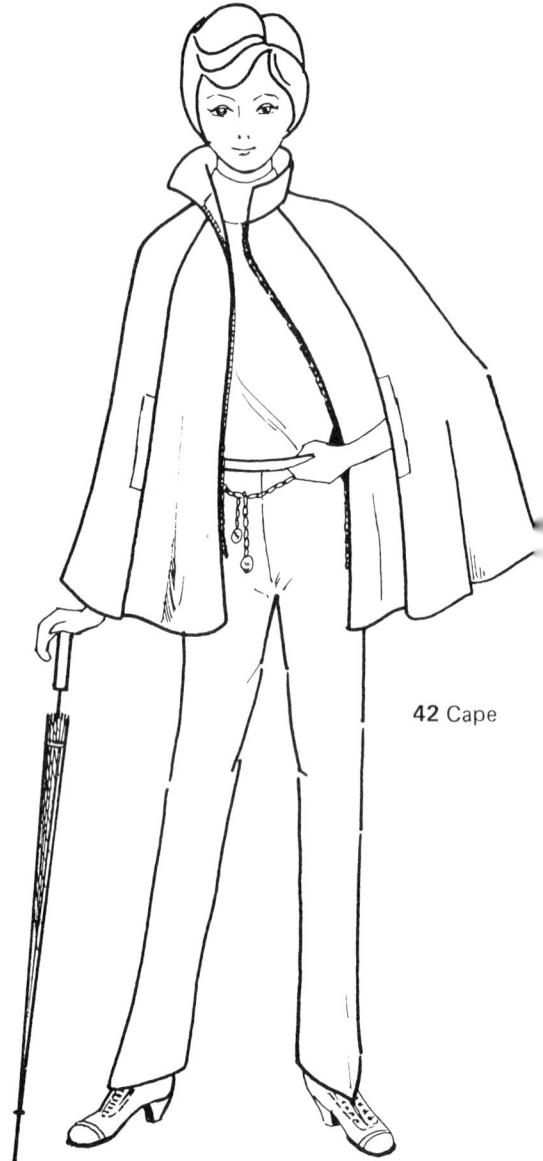

42 Cape

42 Cape

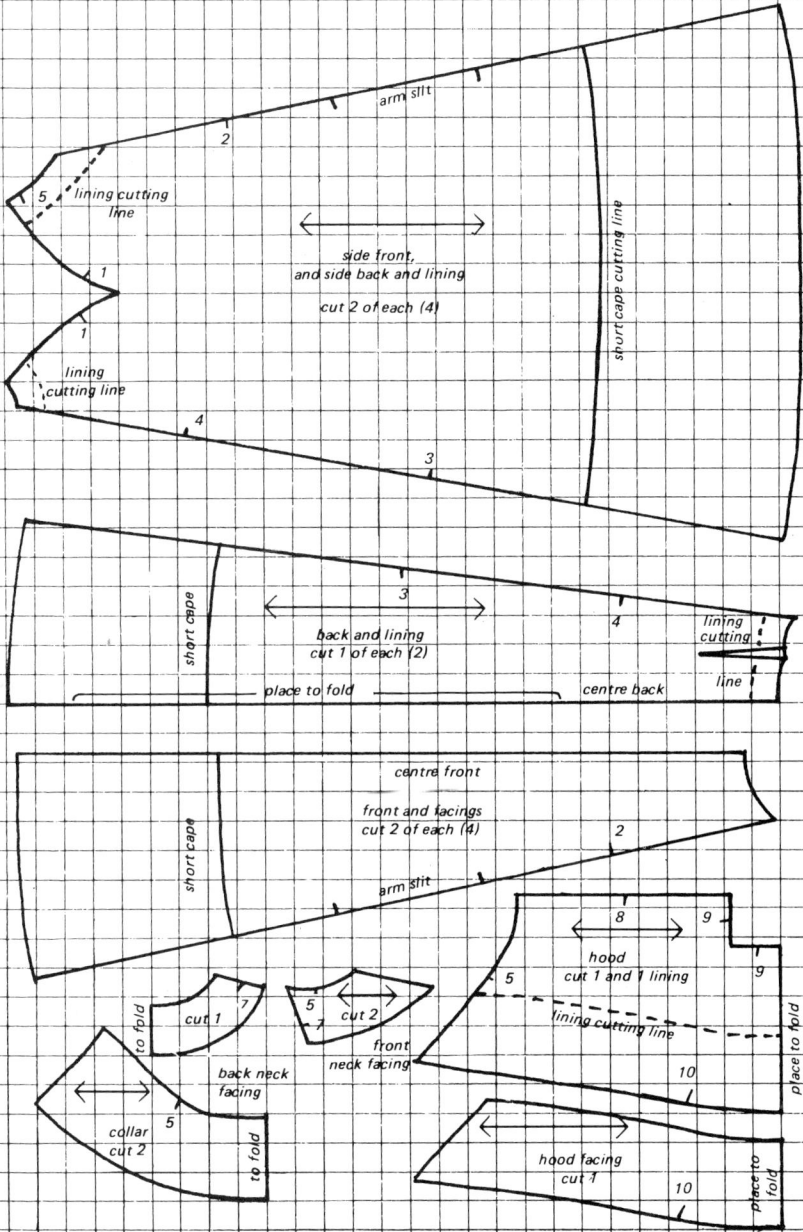

arm slit

2

5　lining cutting line

1

1

lining cutting line

side front, and side back and lining

cut 2 of each (4)

short cape cutting line

4

3

short cape

3

back and lining
cut 1 of each (2)

4

lining cutting line

place to fold

centre back

centre front

front and facings
cut 2 of each (4)

2

short cape

arm slit

hood
cut 1 and 1 lining

8　9

5

9

lining cutting line

to fold

cut 1　7

5　cut 2

front neck facing

10

place to fold

back neck facing

collar cut 2

5

to fold

hood facing
cut 1

place to fold

10

of hood and press. Join hood facing to hood lining and make up as for outer hood. The two hoods are joined to the cape and lining exactly as (but instead of) the two collars.

Turn up outer cape bottom hem, tack and slip-stitch. Press.

If you are having a zip-fastening cape, separate the open-ended zip into two halves. Place the two cape right sides together, and pin up the fronts and round the edge of the hood or collar, matching notches 10, neck seams, etc. Insert one half of the zip into each centre front seam *exactly* opposite one another, all three edges (cape, zip and facing) *in line together*. Tack firmly. Stitch carefully all round. Turn right side out.

Pull out the seam edge and the zip to the stitching. Pin, tack and carefully press.

Cut off surplus at bottom of facings and turn up the edge. Hand-hem into place.

Cut off surplus lining, turn up, pin, try on to check it is not pulling or hanging down, and slip-stitch neatly in place.

Match up inner and outer arm slits. They should coincide exactly *if* you worked to the markings. Pin, tack, and invisibly oversew together.

Top-stitch up the front, round the hood edge (or collar) and down the front, to hold the zip into position. Top-stitch round the arm slits. Tie off all ends and dispose of them by threading them inside the material layers. Press very carefully.

Note 'Frogging' or 'tabs' are applied instead of the zip fastener after the final top-stitching. Buttons and buttonholes are also added at this stage.

Bags

The collection of bags described here covers a lot of uses. The pretty Dorothy bag (pattern 43) was made to carry with the blue silk party dress; the lining is of the same blue silk and the outside is of blue velvet the same colour as the shoulder straps. The knitting bag (pattern 44) was made of three different oddments of material but can, of course, be made of one piece and can be decorated however you like. The saddle bag style of shoulder bag (pattern 45) was two-coloured, made from the same fabric as the hooded coat, and from the same material used to make the straight skirt. More left-overs, in fact! The second shoulder bag (pattern 46) was made of patchwork, using small scrap pieces of suede in a variety of colours, butted together and secured with close zig-zag stitch, but of course, it can be made of any strong material.

Shopping bag 47 was a colourful combination of striped and plain, very tough polyester jersey. Shopping bag 48, which took much longer to make and was rather more expensive, was of canvas, embroidered with thick wool, lined with waterproof nylon, with plaited wool handles. We used up scrap wool to make a tartan-style pattern in petit point, but there are many other canvas stitches, and it is fun to make your own design. The beach or games bag (pattern 49) proved to be a true hold-all! It was made of brightly striped, coarse, cotton-type material with a layer of stiffening and a waterproof nylon lining, but the lining can be loose and some materials do not need stiffening. The fabric does, however, need to be robust.

43 'Dorothy' bag

See p. 78 for pattern pieces. Join the two outside pieces to the two inside top strips along the long edge, then the lining to the bottom edge of the inner top pieces, right sides together. Press. Join the resulting two pieces together, leaving a gap of 4 cm from X – X. Press flat. Reinforce by stitching down seam round those gaps. Press. Fold down the inner top strips and attached lining to meet the bottom edge of the bag and press. Tack and stitch around the bag just above the join of bag and lining. Repeat 2 cm above, and a further 2 cm above. This gives the two channels for the drawstrings, which should coincide with the gaps left in the side seams.

Round the bottom edge, stitch a 1 cm (double) dart every 2 cm. In this way you lose 2 cm every 2 cm. Or, alternatively, make a 1 cm double pleat every 2 cm. This reduces the measurement round the bag bottom edge to approximately that of the circumference of the bag base. Pin, easing the two edges of bag and base together, tack and stitch.

Cut out a circle of rigid cardboard about 1.5 cm less in diameter than the base. Then, using Copydex or similar adhesive, stick it inside the base circle of the bag. Turn in a hem round the outside edge of the lining base, pin and hand-stitch it into position over the cardboard and the circular join.

49 Beach or games bag

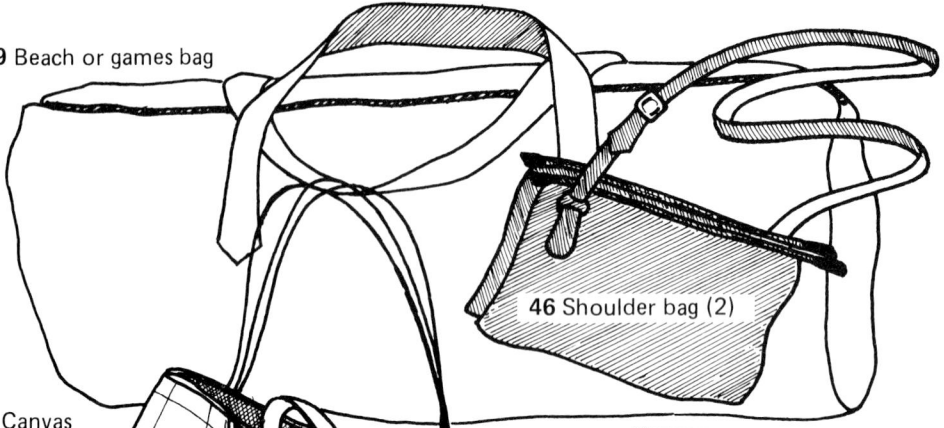

46 Shoulder bag (2)

48 Canvas
Shopping bag

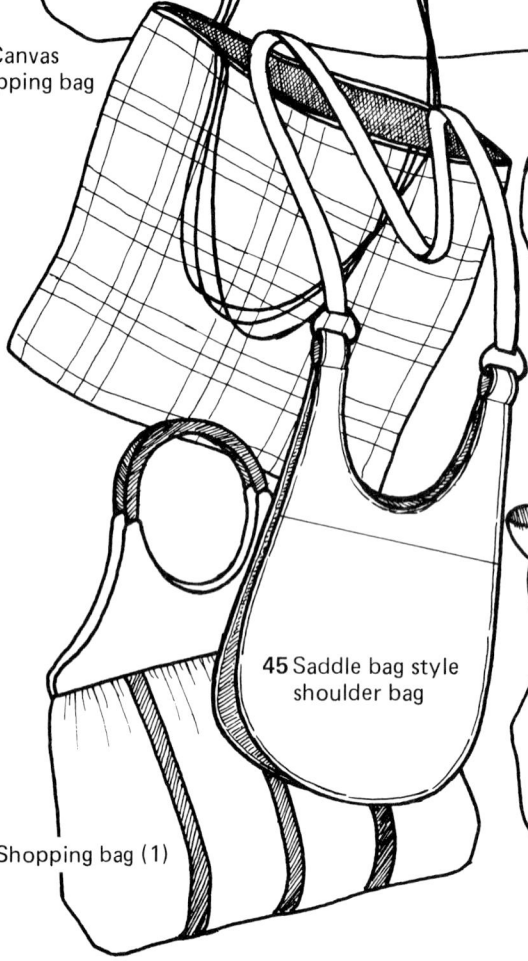

44 Knitting or
work bag

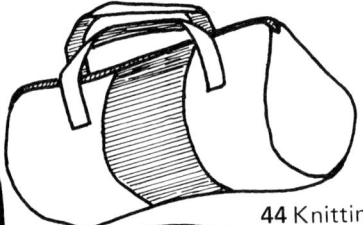

45 Saddle bag style
shoulder bag

43 'Dorothy'
bag

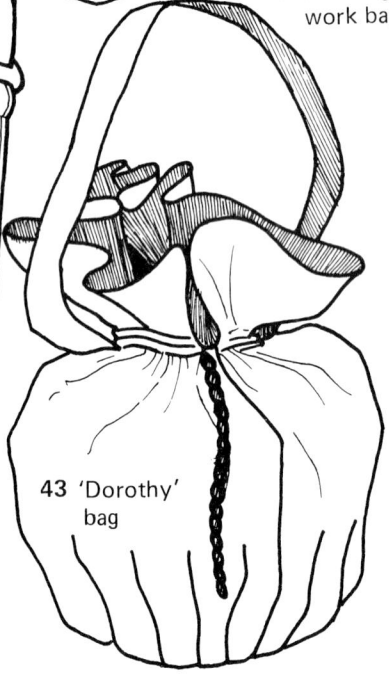

47 Shopping bag (1)

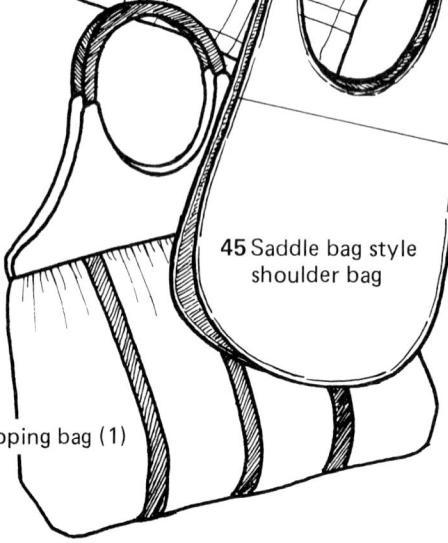

Make the handle, turn right side out, stitch ends neatly, pin into position on side seams above drawstring channels and stitch securely.

Thread two cords, or material ties, through the two channels from opposite sides. Tie or stitch ends together. Pull up and knot together to hold.

44 Knitting or work bag

See p. 78 for pattern pieces. Make the two handles, turning right sides out and stitching up both ends neatly. Position as shown on the pattern and stitch securely into place.

Put the zip fastener right sides together between the two short edges of the pieces of material. Tack and stitch. Press on the right side and top-stitch either side of zip.

Turn inside-out. With right sides together, ease the bag ends to the bag long edges. Tack and stitch. Neaten the edges. If wanted, a lining can be made and stitched by hand to the back of the zip.

45 Saddle bag style shoulder bag

See p. 78 for pattern pieces. Reinforce the lower half of each of the bag pieces with iron on adhesive interlining.

Cut across the inner half of the bag where the dotted lines are sited. Turn in a hem on either side of both cuts. Tack in two zips to fit across, and stitch neatly and securely. Press. It should be the same size again as the outer half.

Fold the inner bag piece in half, zip positions matching, with right sides together, and stitch them together as indicated by the horseshoe dotted line. Reinforce start and finish and tie off very securely.

Place a lining piece over each half of the inner bag. Turn a hem in and stitch to the lower edge of each zip. Place the other two lining pieces flat over these, then the outer bag piece exactly over the linings. Pin and tack inner and outer pieces and lining edges together all round the outside and the inner edge, and stitch to hold.

Machine a line of stitching through inner and outer pieces of the bags, just above both zips, to stabilise the body of the bag and secure the upper edge of the linings that were not stitched to the zip.

Bind the inner and outer edges of both halves of the bag with braid.

Make the shoulder strap and two short, reinforced lengths of fabric for the loops. If you can obtain two big split rings to slide over the upper folds of the bag, they are more convenient. Thread one end of the shoulder strap through one ring or loop, and stitch over; adjust the other end to fit comfortably, cut off surplus and stitch that end over also.

46 Shoulder bag (2)

See p. 78 for pattern pieces. This bag is also made in two halves. Join three sides of inner and outer pieces of both halves, with right sides together. Turn right sides out and press. Put in zip fasteners, and top-stitch.

Make linings in the same way, put inside the bags and stitch to the lower edge of the zips.

With the zips wide open, pin the two halves of the bag together through the inner pieces and carefully stitch from the edge of the zips in a rectangle about 2 cm smaller than the bags, round three edges and back to the zip. Reinforce start and finish. Tie off securely. This gives a third pocket.

Make tabs. Fold in half through a D-ring and stitch to top left hand quarter of outer sides of the twin bags.

Make shoulder strap. Pass one end through D-ring and stitch down. Adjust the other end to fit comfortably, and cut off surplus before stitching down.

Note If you are unable to get D-rings, the shoulder strap can be stitched straight onto the bag. Double shoulder straps can be made if preferred.

43 'Dorothy' bag **44** Knitting or work bag **45** Saddle bag style shoulder bag
46 Shoulder bag (2) **47** Shopping bag **48** Canvas shopping bag **49** Beach or games bag

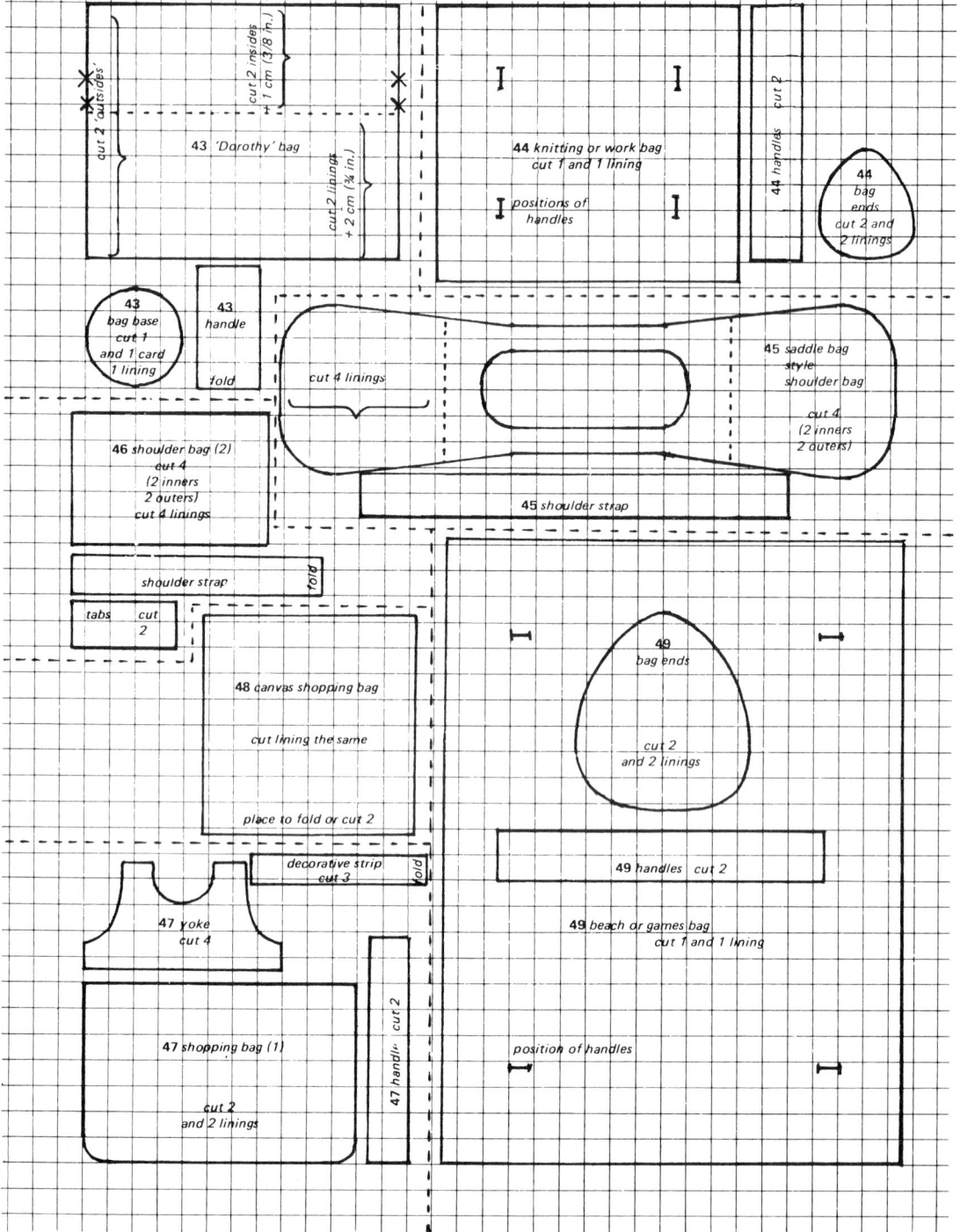

cut 2 insides + 1 cm (3/8 in.)

cut 2 'outsides'

43 'Dorothy' bag

cut 2 linings + 2 cm (3/4 in.)

44 knitting or work bag
cut 1 and 1 lining

positions of handles

44 handles cut 2

44 bag ends cut 2 and 2 linings

43 bag base cut 1 and 1 card 1 lining

43 handle

fold

cut 4 linings

45 saddle bag style shoulder bag

cut 4 (2 inners 2 outers)

46 shoulder bag (2) cut 4 (2 inners 2 outers) cut 4 linings

45 shoulder strap

shoulder strap

fold

tabs cut 2

48 canvas shopping bag

cut lining the same

place to fold or cut 2

49 bag ends

cut 2 and 2 linings

decorative strip cut 3

fold

49 handles cut 2

47 yoke cut 4

49 beach or games bag cut 1 and 1 lining

47 shopping bag (1)

cut 2 and 2 linings

47 handle cut 2

position of handles

78

47   Shopping bag (1)

See p. 78 for pattern pieces. With right sides together, join the two main halves of the bag together round three sides. Turn right side out and press. Make the lining likewise. Put it inside the bag and stitch together round the top edge.

Join the two short sides (notches 2) of inner and outer yokes.

Turn in a hem on each long edge of the handles and bring the hems together, enclosing a length of old clothes line in each, about 3 cm shorter than the handle. Then double-stitch the hem edges.

With right sides together, and enclosing the handles, place handle ends in line with the 'shoulder' of the yokes, pin, tack and stitch all round the top edge of the bag yokes. Turn right side out and press. This brings the handles to the outside in two matching rounded loops.

Pleat or gather the top edges of the bag to fit the bottom edge of the yoke. Matching side seams and centres, with right sides together, pin, tack and stitch outer yoke to main bag. Press seam upwards. Turn in hem along bottom of inner yoke and pin, tack and closely hand-hem it to the line of machining visible. Press.

Top-stitch all round edges of the yoke.

Note The bands in the pattern are optional, and are applied after joining the two bottom edges together and before the sides are joined.

48   Canvas shopping bag

See p. 78 for pattern pieces. The piece of canvas should be 68 x 34 mm and, when it is embroidered, the pattern should come to within approximately 1 cm of both long edges and 2 cm of the two short edges.

Fold the canvas in half and join up the sides. Turn right sides out and press. Also join the sides of the lining and place it inside the bag. Stitch together round the top.

Take a strip of suede, firm-weave fabric, or wide braid, and bind the top edge of the bag to cover canvas edge.

Make six cords, three for each handle, by plaiting together lengths of the wool used for embroidering the bag.

Lay the ends of the three cords side by side, stitch them several times across to half a small piece of suede or binding fabric. Fold and stick the other half of the suede over the end using Copydex. Then stitch these tabs in place, along the top of the bag.

49   Beach or games bag

Make up the bag in exactly the same way as given in the instructions for the knitting bag (pattern 44).

Soft toys and table linen

The toys and 'knick-knacks', shown here were almost all made from scrap bits of material, wool, leather and stuffing. I used an old T-shirt, for example, for the body of the rag doll. They were intended to be presents for younger members of the family, but quite often ended up being kept by those who made them. The table 'linen' is easy, useful and should delight mothers, aunts and grandmothers!

Unless otherwise stated, all seams in this project are stitched with right sides together and should be about 7-8 mm wide, except in felt when they should be 4 mm.

50 'Daisy Jane' rag doll

See p. 82 for pattern pieces. Stitch darts in both halves of the head front. Press. Stitch centre front seam of the head (notch 1). Clip curve and press.

With Copydex, firmly stick black pupil of each eye to blue iris, and these to the whites of the eyes. Work a small white highlight on each pupil with two or three satin-stitches, in embroidery silk. Stick whites of eyes to positions marked on the pattern, then work a line of very small black chain-stitch over extreme edge, all round. Work eyelashes with black stem-stitching, and eyebrows with diagonal satin-stitch, stretching to stem-stitch towards outer ends.

Stitch lips in place, then hand-hem, with very tiny stitches, all round, with matching Sylko.

Then work a line of stem-stitch across middle of mouth in Sylko.

Make two French knots for nostrils with black or brown embroidery silk.

Join centre back head seam (notches 12 and 13), leaving a gap between the two dots. Clip and press flat.

Join side seams (notch 2) of front and back head. Clip and press. Turn right side out.

Join centre back of body, leaving a gap between the two dots. Press. Stitch back left and right arm to body back, matching notches 3. Join front left and right arm to body front, matching notches 3. Press the four seams outwards.

Stitch from neck edge all round arms, down to hip edge on both sides. Clip all curves and corners carefully and turn right sides out. Turn in a hem of about 1 cm round body bottom edge and down round the neck edge.

Join the inner curve of each footpiece to the bottom of each leg with right sides facing and notches 4 matching. Clip carefully and press. Join the seam of each leg and back foot (notch 5), leaving a gap between the two dots. Press, with seam at the back of each leg.

With right sides together, join soles to feet edges, matching notches 6.

Place the tops of each leg inside the bottom turning of the body, with backs and fronts matching. Stitch right across and tie off ends securely. This provides the bending hip joints of the doll.

Place the neck edge of the head inside the

50 'Daisy Jane' rag doll (1 sq. = 1 cm)

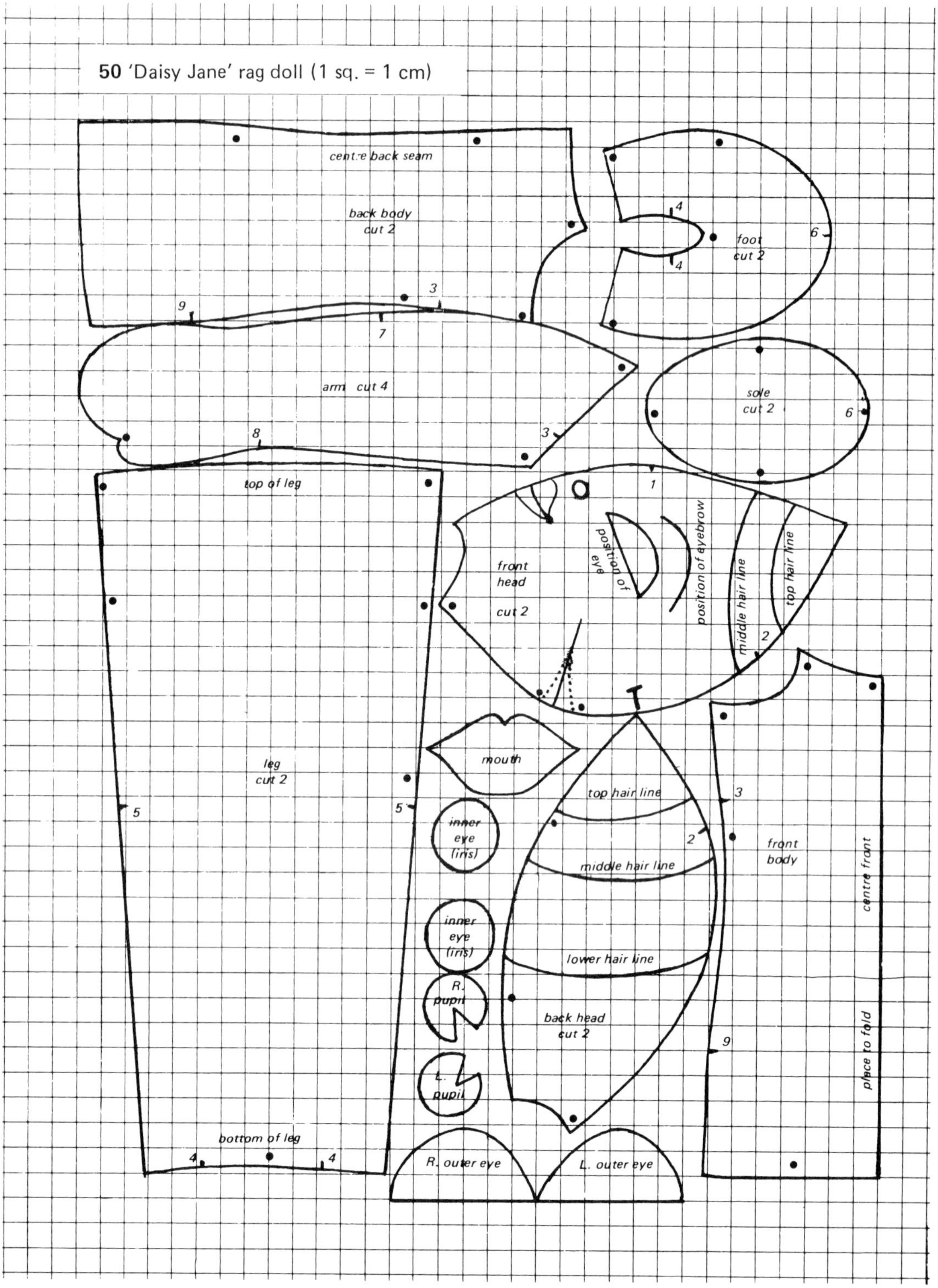

centre back seam

back body
cut 2

foot
cut 2

4

4

6

9

3

7

arm cut 4

3

sole
cut 2

6

8

3

top of leg

front
head
cut 2

1

position of eye

position of eyebrow

middle hair line

top hair line

2

leg
cut 2

mouth

top hair line

3

5

5

inner
eye
(iris)

middle hair line

2

front
body

inner
eye
(iris)

lower hair line

R.
pupil

back head
cut 2

9

centre front

L.
pupil

bottom of leg

4

4

R. outer eye

L. outer eye

place to fold

50a Clothes for rag doll

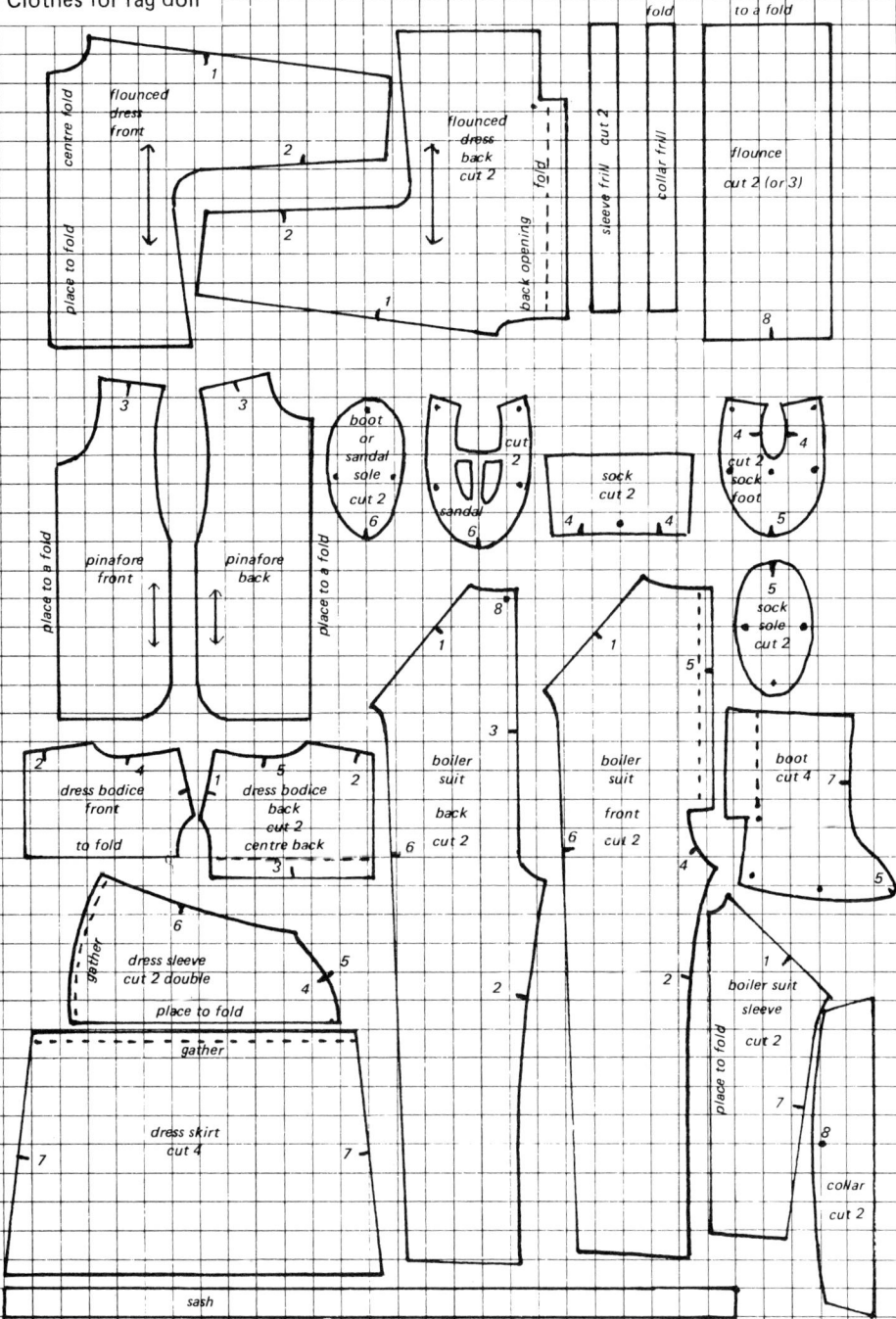

flounced
dress
front

centre fold

place to fold

1

2

2

1

flounced
dress
back
cut 2

fold

back opening

sleeve frill cut 2

collar frill

fold

to a fold

flounce
cut 2 (or 3)

8

3

3

pinafore
front

pinafore
back

place to a fold

place to a fold

boot
or
sandal
sole
cut 2

6

sandal

cut
2

6

sock
cut 2

4

4

4

4

cut 2
sock
foot

2

5

5
sock
sole
cut 2

2

4

dress bodice
front

to fold

1

5

dress bodice
back
cut 2
centre back

2

3

boiler
suit

back

cut 2

8

1

3

2

6

boiler
suit

front

cut 2

1

5

6

4

boot
cut 4

7

5

gather

dress sleeve
cut 2 double

place to fold

6

5

4

gather

dress skirt
cut 4

7

7

sash

boiler suit
sleeve
cut 2

place to fold

1

2

7

8

collar
cut 2

83

neck turning of the body. Pin, tack and hand-hem all round, using small neat stitches, and securely tie off ends.

With the help of a stuffing stick or a knitting needle, stuff feet and legs up to hips via the gaps in back leg seams. Close the openings with small, neat ladder-stitch, fastening off carefully. Stuff the arms and stitch across the top to give the shoulder joint movement, then the body up to the neck. Close the back seam securely, stuff the neck and head and close the head seam.

Cut two strips of straight, narrow binding or string, the length from the centre front parting, across the forehead, down the side of the face and round the nape of the neck to the centre back, and two pieces the length from the centre front, along the parting down to the centre back of the neck. Cut lengths of thick wool about 48 cm long. Fold them in half over the binding or string to make a close double fringe and then stitch wool securely to it. Pin the lengths of fringed binding or string in place round the hairline and parting. Gather into bunches on either side to check if 'scalp' is covered. If not, repeat process with a second line of fringed binding just inside the position of the first. Arrange the 'hair' to form bunches either side of the head. Tie with ribbon bows. Trim odd ends.

For a fringed hair style, cut 16 cm of straight binding and stitch 5 cm long strands of wool closely along the binding. Stitch binding to 'lower' hairline on doll's head. Then cut 27 cm of binding or string and stitch 8 cm long strands of wool closely for 9 cm at each end, and 4 cm long strands to the centre 9 cm. Stitch to middle hair line with short strands at front. Then cut 18 cm of binding or string, and 33 cm long strands of wool. Stitch the binding to the closely placed strands of wool 11 cm from the bottom end (22 cm from the top). Stitch the binding to the top hair line, short ends of wool downwards. Gather long ends in pony tail on top of head, and tie securely. Allow ponytail to fall evenly over head. Trim, to follow line of fringe and lower edge of wool from the middle hair line.

Note On p. 83 there is a sheet of patterns for two dresses, an apron, socks and shoes, boots and a boiler suit, but these can be adapted in any way you choose.

50 Daisy Jane rag doll

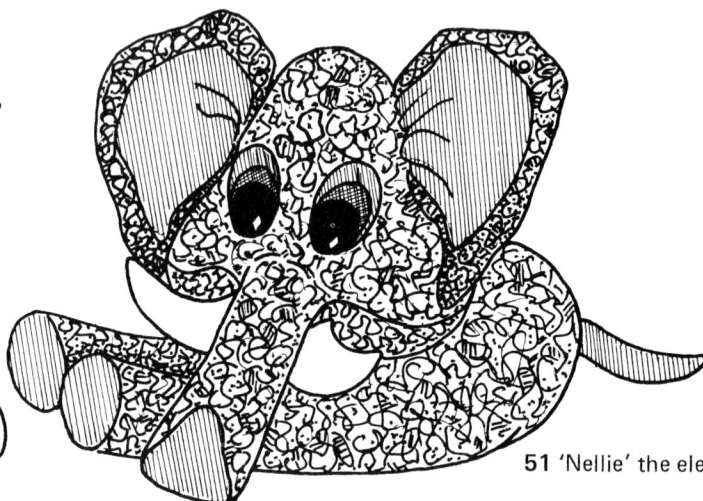

51 'Nellie' the elephant

51 'Nellie' the elephant

See p. 86 for pattern pieces. Inner ears, trunk, and soles of feet are made from coloured felt; tusks, whites of eyes and pupil highlights are made from white felt; irises are in green felt; and pupils and toe nails from black felt. The rest was cut out from gaily coloured curtain fabric.

Note Join all pieces with right sides together and, unless stated otherwise, the seam allowance is about 8 mm.

Assemble eyes as for rag doll, but with felt highlights and, if possible, stitch eyes into the position indicated on the pattern with machine satin-stitch about 3 mm wide in black Sylko, to give a good outline. Then join head pieces from upper tip of trunk to point A. Pin head to back of head piece matching up points B on each side.

Pin pieces together from B to C and C to A, easing the fabric edges together to match centre back and seam on head piece.

Working again from B, pin back of head piece round the bulge of the cheek to E. Machine all this but leave a 10 cm gap at the centre back for mouth as shown on pattern. Clip curves and turn right sides out.

Stitch the three darts in the end of the trunk piece to form a triangle. Stitch dart in under trunk piece, fold D to E and oversew. This makes the mouth opening. Join end of trunk piece to trunk and under trunk, round all three sides. Join under trunk to trunk matching E and F. Turn right side out.

Join tusks in pairs, leaving ends open. Turn right sides out, stuff, and stitch to close ends.

Stitch inner ears into place on outside of front half of each ear. Then stitch the ear pieces together in pairs, leaving bottoms open. Clip curves and turn right sides out. Cut two ears about 1 cm less all round, from thin foam sheet, and insert into each ear. Turn in raw edges and slip-stitch together, pulling thread up tight to gather slightly.

Stitch dart on inner leg piece. Join underbody to inner leg piece, along inside edge, following the curve. Clip. Join side legs to inner legs' piece, matching V and W.

Join body pieces from X to Y taking a good 13 mm seam. Match points Z and stitch from Z up to centre front dart, joining legs to body, but leaving neck open for stuffing.

From underbody pattern, cut out a piece of stiff card, omitting legs. Trim off 13 cm all round. Stitch underbody to body round edges, leaving gap to insert card base. Clip curves, turn right side out, insert card and stitch to close gap.

Join tail pieces, leaving end open. Turn right side out, stuff, turn in raw edge, slip-stitch to close and attach firmly to body with ladder-stitch.

Turn in lower edges of legs and pin soles in place. Oversew, easing felt to give a rounded effect.

Stuff the body, pushing the card down firmly first; close the opening neatly and securely.

Stuff head firmly. Turn in raw edges and slip-stitch to under trunk, inserting tusks between felt and fabric. Push down surplus left for mouth.

Glue toe pieces in place. Stitch ears in position.

Position head on body, so that trunk rests on the legs. With strong double thread, stitch head securely to body.

52 'Dracula' the bloodhound

See p. 87 for pattern pieces. For a small dog (27 cm long and 15 cm tall), 1 square equals 1 cm. For a larger dog (54 cm long and 30 cm tall), 1 square equals 2 cm. The ears, nose, tongue and eyes were of felt, the rest of the dog of strong printed cotton. 6 mm seams are allowed. All cotton pieces are sewn right sides together with small stitches, and curves are carefully clipped before turning right sides out to stuff.

Stitch head gusset to face gusset, A to A, at forehead. Stitch face gusset to underbody gusset, D to D, at throat.

Place head and body pieces together. Pin completed gussets in between, carefully matching AA, BB, CC and DD and stitch all

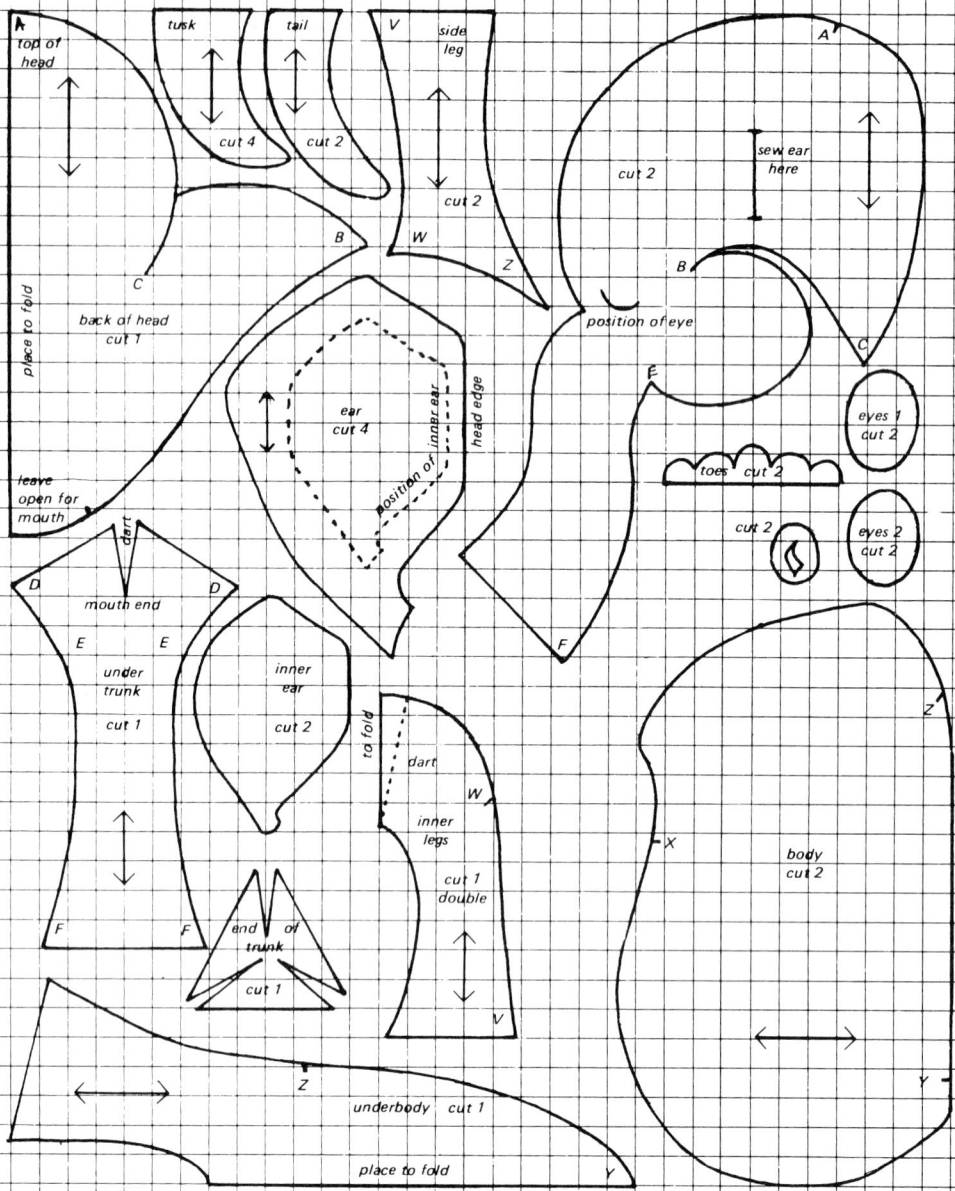

top of head

tusk

tail

V side leg

A

cut 4

cut 2

cut 2

cut 2

sew ear here

B

W

Z

B

position of eye

C

back of head cut 1

C

place to fold

ear cut 4

head edge

position of inner ear

E

toes cut 2

eyes 1 cut 2

F

cut 2

eyes 2 cut 2

leave open for mouth

dart

D

D

mouth end

E

E

under trunk

cut 1

inner ear

cut 2

to fold

dart

W

inner legs

cut 1 double

X

body cut 2

Z

F

F

end of trunk

cut 1

V

Z

underbody cut 1

place to fold

Y

Y

51 Nellie the elephant
(1 sq. = 2 cm)

86

52 'Dracula' the bloodhound (1 sq. = 1 cm) **53a** Baby ball (1 sq. = 0.5 cm)
53b 'Portly' pig (1 sq. = 0.5 cm) **53c** 'French Fred' frog (1 sq. = 0.5 cm)

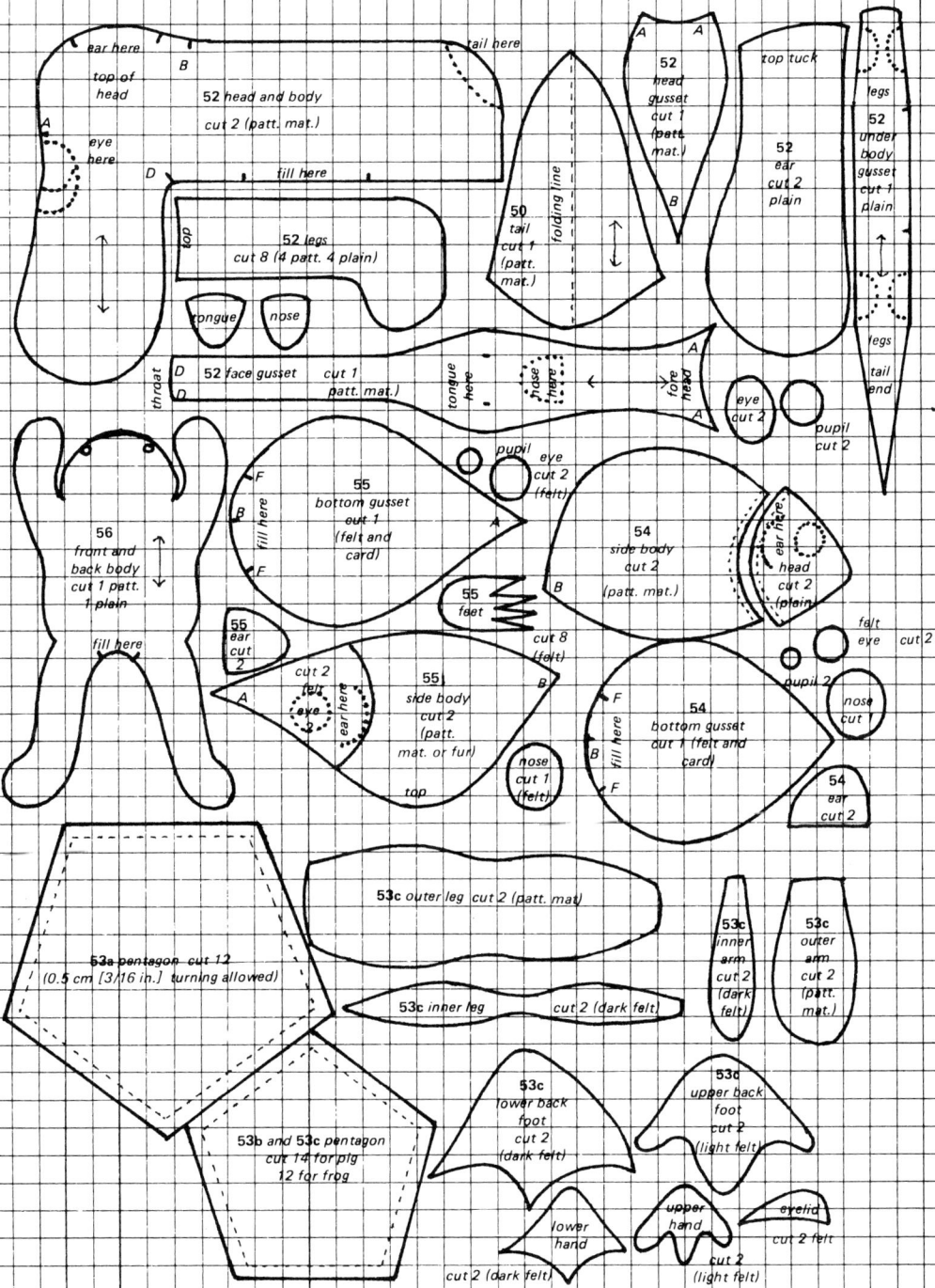

ear here

top of head

B

tail here

A A

52 *head gusset cut 1 (patt. mat.)*

top tuck

legs

A

eye here

52 *head and body cut 2 (patt. mat.)*

52 *ear cut 2 plain*

52 *under body gusset cut 1 plain*

D

fill here

B

50 *tail cut 1 (patt. mat.)*

folding line

top

52 *legs cut 8 (4 patt. 4 plain)*

tongue

nose

A

legs

throat

D

52 *face gusset* cut 1 *patt. mat.)*

D

tongue here

nose here

fore head

A

eye cut 2

tail end

pupil cut 2

F

B

fill here

F

55 *bottom gusset cut 1 (felt and card)*

pupil *eye cut 2 (felt)*

A

54 *side body cut 2 (patt. mat.)*

B

ear here

54 *head cut 2 plain*

56 *front and back body cut 1 patt. 1 plain*

55 *ear cut 2*

cut 2 felt *eye 2*

ear here

55 *feet*

55 *side body cut 2 (patt. mat. or fur)*

B

cut 8 (felt)

felt eye cut 2

fill here

A

F

B

fill here

F

54 *bottom gusset cut 1 (felt and card)*

pupil 2

nose cut

54 *ear cut 2*

nose cut 1 (felt)

F

top

53c *outer leg cut 2 (patt. mat)*

53c *inner arm cut 2 (dark felt)*

53c *outer arm cut 2 (patt. mat.)*

53a *pentagon cut 12* (0.5 cm [3/16 in.] turning allowed)

53c *inner leg* cut 2 (dark felt)

53c *lower back foot cut 2 (dark felt)*

53c *upper back foot cut 2 (light felt)*

53b and 53c *pentagon cut 14 for pig 12 for frog*

lower hand cut 2 (dark felt)

upper hand cut 2 (light felt)

eyelid cut 2 felt

54 'Mighty Mouse' pincushion (1 sq. = 1 or 2 cm) **55** 'Horace' hedgehog (J.B.C. mole) (1 sq. = 1 or 2 cm)
56 'Fearless' the floppy frog (1 sq. = 1 or 2 cm)

round, but leave a gap for stuffing at one side of underbody gusset seam. Stitch across back of dog from B to C. Clip, turn, stuff and stitch up gap.

Stitch leg pieces together, in pairs round three sides, leaving tops open. Clip, turn, stuff and run a gathering thread round top edge. Draw up a little, and making sure feet are pointing forward, stitch legs to position indicated on underbody gusset, using small close stitches and making sure legs are firmly secured.

With Copydex, stick pupils to whites of each eye (a brown iris, slightly bigger than the pupil can be included if you wish). Work a small white highlight on each pupil with embroidery silk and two or three satin-stitches. Stick and stitch whites of eyes in position. A line of black, very small chain stitch round them, emphasises the eyes.

Stick and hand-hem invisibly into place the nose and the straight edge of tongue so that it points forward.

turn in a small hem round open end and stitch firmly to body where indicated, so that tail is in a straight continuous line with the back.

53 Toys made with pentagons

See p. 87 for pattern pieces. 1 square equals 0.5 cm.

53(a) Baby ball

An ideal, soft, washable, safe toy for a baby. It *can* be made in different coloured felts, but to be completely washable, cut twelve pentagons from different, strong, closely woven scrap fabrics. Join six of them as in diagrams 1 and 2

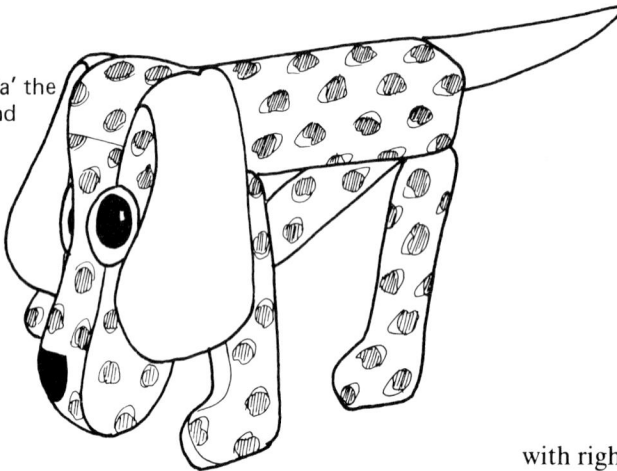

53a Baby ball

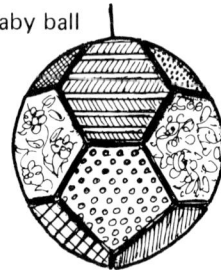

52 'Dracula' the bloodhound

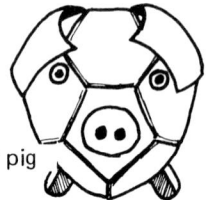

53b 'Portly' pig

Make a small pleat at the top of each ear, stick or stitch to hold, then stitch each ear very firmly and securely to the seams on either side of top of head as indicated.

Fold the tail in half lengthwise, F to F. Stitch from F to E. Turn right sides out, stuff, then

with right sides together and, using a very small machine-stitch, zig-zag over the raw edges. Repeat with the other six patches. Still with right sides together, join the two halves together leaving one side unstitched. Turn right side out and stuff firmly with man-made wadding or foam crumbs, pushing and prodding to get a true ball. Stitch up gap with tiny, close oversewing.

53(b) 'Portly' pig

Use felt for the pig or soft suede or leather. Join with stab-stitch on the outside, to give small ridges. Cut fourteen pentagons of the smaller size.

Make the body and stuff in the same way as the ball.

Stick the four nose pieces together, and stitch the two nostrils with small satin-stitches (diagram 3). Stick firmly to the face as shown in diagram 4.

Stitch two black beads in positions indicated, passing needle through the head and pulling 'eyes' slightly together (diagram 4).

Gather one side of the two remaining pentagons and tie off securely (diagram 5). Oversew in position where indicated (diagram 4).

Cut four strips of felt or leather 5 x 6 mm. Spread Copydex on one side of each and roll up tight for legs, (diagram 6). Sew ends to secure, and then embroider a cloven hoof mark on each foot. Stick and stitch the legs to the position indicated diagrams 4 and 7. Take half a pipe cleaner and a strip of felt or leather 9 x 1.3 cm. Fold the fabric tightly round the pipe cleaner and stitch firmly shaping to a point at one end. Wind pipe cleaner round a pencil to curl it, and stitch the blunt end firmly to body where indicated (diagram 7).

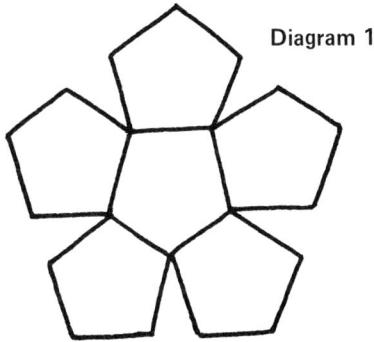
Diagram 1

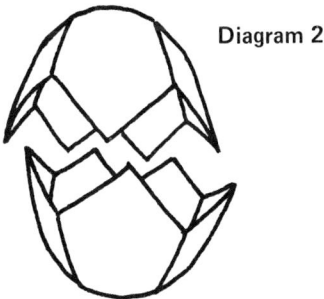
Diagram 4

Diagram 5 (ear)

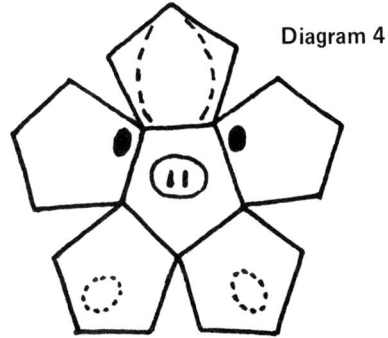
Diagram 6 (legs)

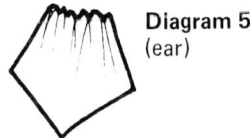
Diagram 2

Diagram 7

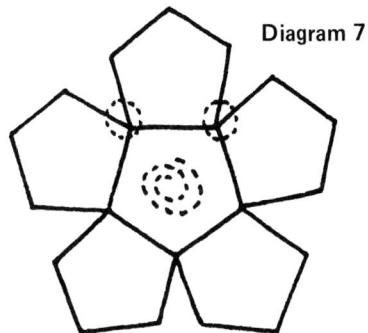
Diagram 3 (nose)

53(c) 'French Fred' frog

Cut 12 pentagons of felt, fabric, leather, velvet, etc., or combinations of two or three of these. Study the illustration to decide how you want to distribute the fabrics, but notice that feet and inner legs and arms are easier to cope with if done in strong, non-fraying material.

Make up body as described for (a) and (b).

Stitch two black beads in position, as in (b), then stitch the eyelids in place, (diagram 8).

Take two pipe cleaners. Bend one up 3.8 cm from end. Wrap a little cotton wool round remainder and hold in place with thread wound round it (diagram 9). Take leg piece A, lay

Take remaining two pipe cleaners, cut them in half, use two lengths to make front legs (bending up 2.5 cm for claw) and the other two to make the rest of the claws, using the same method as for the back legs.

Stitch front and back legs securely in place as indicated on diagrams 8 and 12.

Stitch mouth in stem-stitch. Bend legs to the positions you want. Perhaps suspend 'Fred' on a cord.

55c 'French Fred' Frog

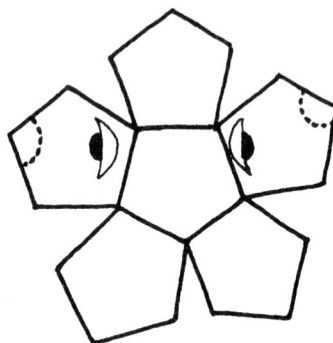

Diagram 8

Diagram 9   Diagram 10   Diagram 11

padded part of pipe cleaner down middle of wrong side. Turn edges over it (turn a small hem, if fraying fabric, on top edge) and stitch together, and also turn in bottom edge and stitch.

Take another pipe cleaner, cut 11.5 cm off it, and twist it round end of the pipe cleaner protruding from leg piece, to form a claw (diagram 10). Place one lower back foot piece below the claw, and one upper back foot piece above it. Sew round the claw with running stitch as in diagram 11, to form a webbed foot. Sew it to the lower leg edge. Sew inner leg piece B over the rather rough seam down the back of the leg, with neat, even stitches. Repeat whole process for the other back leg.

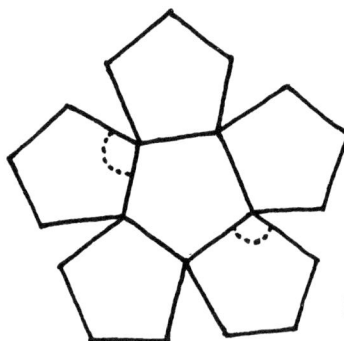

Diagram 12

54 'Mighty Mouse' pincushion

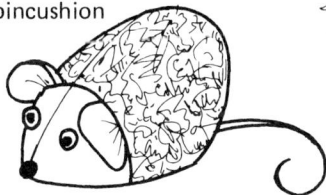

See p. 87 for pattern pieces. One square equals 1 or 2 cm. Make the body of pretty, strong, cotton fabric, with the head and underside of felt.

Join head pieces' centre front seam, then the two side body pieces, centre front to back. Clip, press. Turn right sides out. Join head to body, matching seams. Clip, press and turn right side out.

Cut a cardboard base 5 mm smaller than the pattern of the bottom gusset. Join body to felt bottom gusset, easing edges together. Leave a gap to insert (a) the cardboard base, and having pushed that firmly down and threaded through a cord tail, (b) the stuffing. (Kapok, polyester filling, sawdust etc., are all suitable – whichever you feel keeps your pins and needles dry, bright and rustless.)

55 'Horace' hedgehog ('J.C.B.' mole)

See p. 87 for pattern pieces. One square = 1 or 2 cm. These two delightful little animals are made from the same pattern. 'J.C.B.' has a smooth, short-fur body, while 'Horace' has long 'spikes' made by using long-haired fur or fur fabric, or by making close wool loops to cover his body and then cutting them. Hair spray is useful to hold the 'spikes', especially in fur.

The method of working is exactly the same as for 'Mighty Mouse', but there is no tail, and the feet are stuck together in pairs and stitched to the bottom edge of the body in the proper position.

56 'Fearless' the floppy frog

See p. 87 for pattern pieces. One square equals 1 or 2 cm. Cut back piece patterned, and front piece, plain.

55 'Horace' hedgehog ('J.C.B.' mole)

54 'Mighty Mouse' pincushion

56 'Fearless' the floppy frog

Assemble eyes as in other toys (although beads and/or sequins may be used for the iris and pupil) and stick and stitch them in place, along with nose and ears. Draw up the edge of the nose and stuff to get a firm, round 'knob', before sticking and firmly stitching it down. Thread stiff nylon line or thread 'whiskers' through from side to side, catch with a single stitch each side to prevent them being pulled out.

With right sides together, join all round, with a small machine-stitch, leaving an unstitched gap as indicated. Clip thoroughly and carefully all curves and corners. Turn right sides out carefully.

Stitch two black beads securely where shown, pulling them together slightly, to give a gently sunken effect.

Make a cardboard cone and pour in rice, beans, or whatever heavy loose filling you choose. The filling must be able to slide and move in and out of legs and arms without sticking.

Stitch up the filling gap securely.

57 Round or oval table-cloth

Many people have round or oval dining tables, but it is quite unusual to come across a round or oval table-cloth. Yet it is very easy to make one, and it would make a good present.

Look for the very wide (60-66 in. or 152-168 cm) polyester fabrics, which are inexpensive and come in every colour, many patterns and are stainproof, easy to wash and need no ironing.

Try to make a newspaper pattern of the table top. If the table is round, all you need is the radius, but an oval table needs a bit more calculation, and a pattern.

Look carefully at the diagram before you cut

58 Table mats

Table mats are another acceptable gift, and are easy and quick to make.

I used 1.3 metres of curtain folk weave 122 cm wide, the loosely woven, textured, washable, non-iron fabric which has such attractive colour blends and varied checked, striped or geometrically patterned reversible designs.

Measure the fabric off accurately, as in the diagram, cutting always along a warp or weft thread.

Fringe each mat by pulling out the threads around it to a depth ranging from 4.5 cm on large mats to 2.5 cm on small mats.

Finally, secure the edge of the fabric by zig-zagging accurately round each mat in a contrasting colour to prevent further fraying and leave the fringe unhampered.

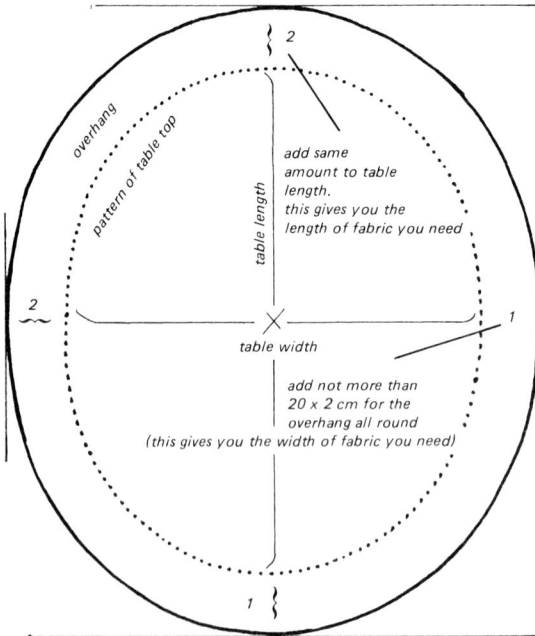

57 Round or oval table-cloth

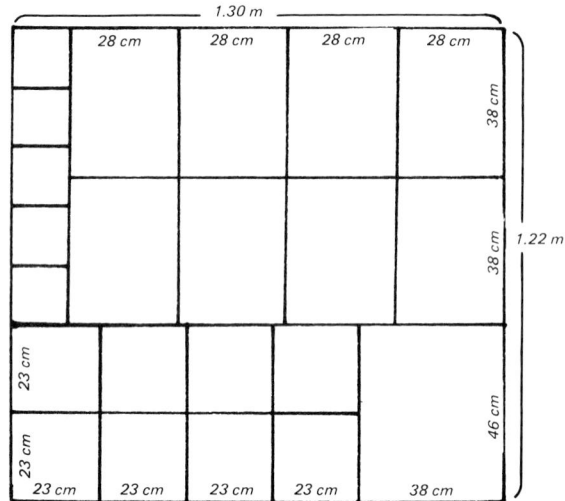

58 Table mats

out the tablecloth. Tack up a very small hem all round the edge, and stitch. A lace edge is an attractive decoration. If you do attach lace, zig-zag it to the edge, and join ends invisibly.

Materials needed for each project

1 Traditional cook's apron and cap
1.50 m of 90 cm (1 m of 152 cm) fabric; Sylko; about 5 m of bias binding (according to length of apron).

2 French cook's apron
2 m of 90 cm (1 m of 152 cm) fabric; Sylko; about 5 m of bias binding.

3 Classic waist apron
70 cm of 90 cm (50 cm of 152 cm) fabric; Sylko; a small piece of contrasting material (optional).

4 Shirt blouse (short sleeves)
1.50 m of 90 cm (1 m of 152 cm) fabric; Sylko; five or six small buttons.

5 High-necked blouse (short sleeves)
1.50 m of 90 cm (1 m of 152 cm) fabric; Sylko; seven small buttons, 1 m narrow velvet ribbon.

6 Magyar-sleeved blouse
1.50 m of 90 cm (1 m of 152 cm) fabric for short sleeves; 3 m of 90 cm (1.50 m of 152 m) (60 in.) fabric for long sleeves; Sylko; four small buttons; 2.5 m bias binding.

7 Long-sleeved, high-necked blouse
2.25 m of 90 cm (1.40 m of 152 cm) fabric; ten small buttons; small piece soft interlining.

8 Straight skirt
1.70 m of 90 cm (75 cm of 152 cm) fabric; 2 cm wide elastic for waist; or waist fastening and 20 cm (8 in.) zip.

9 Four-gored, flared skirt
3.50 m of 90 cm (1.7 m of 152 cm) fabric; Sylko; 20 cm zip; waist fastening; bias binding for hem.

10 Flounced ra-ra skirt
1.20 m of 90 cm (90 cm of 152 cm) fabric; Sylko; waist elastic or 20 cm zip.

11 Pleated ra-ra skirt
As above, but 18 cm zip.

12 Rhumba skirt
2 m of 90 cm (1 m of 152 cm) fabric; Sylko; waist fastening; 15 cm zip.

13 Wrap-over games skirt
1 m of 90 cm (50 cm of 152 cm) fabric; Sylko; two buttons or strip of Velcro.

14 Circular skirt
1 m of 90 cm (1.25 m of 122 cm or 1.50 m of 152 cm) fabric, according to length desired; Sylko; 2 cm wide elastic for waist.

15 Shorts
80 cm of 90 cm (50 cm of 152 cm) fabric; Sylko; 20 cm zip; waist fastening, or 2 cm wide waist elastic.

16 Gathered bikini
1 m of 90 m (75 cm of 152 cm) fabric; Sylko; 4 m narrow elastic.

17 Stretch bikini
70 cm of 90 cm (40 cm of 152 cm) fabric; Sylko; 1.5 m narrow elastic.

18 Chinese pyjamas
3.50 m of 90 cm (1.75 m of 152 cm) fabric; 75 cm of 90 cm (50 cm of 152 cm) fabric for contrast facings; Sylko; elastic for waist, and for (b) jacket, extra length of elastic for waist or reel of shirr-elastic.

19 Kimono
3.75 m of 90 cm (2 m of 152 cm) fabric; 50 cm of 90 cm (25 cm of 152 cm) for contrast facing; Sylko.

20 Housecoat
6.25 m of 90 cm (3.70 m of 152 cm) fabric (1 m and 70 cm respectively can be of contrasting colour); Sylko; four buttons.

21 Nightdress
3 m of 90 cm (1.50 m of 152 cm) fabric; 40 cm lace for outer yoke; Sylko.

22 Bolero
1 m of 90 cm (50 cm of 152 cm) fabric; Sylko; bias binding.

23 Gilet (1)
1.50 m of 90 cm (80 cm of 152 cm) fabric; 1.50 m lining; Sylko.

24 Gilet (2)
As for 23.

25 Pullover
1.50 m of 90 cm (1.40 m of 152 cm) fabric; Sylko.

26 Waistcoat
1 m of 90 cm (60 cm of 152 cm) fabric; Sylko.

27 Overblouse
1 m of 90 cm (70 cm of 152 cm) fabric; Sylko; seven buttons.

28 Zip jacket
2.50 m of 90 cm (1.50 m of 152 cm) fabric; Sylko; 2.50 m lining material; 56-61 cm open-ended zip; 1.50 m wide elastic; stiffening for collar.

29 Hooded, belted jacket
2 m of 152 cm fabric; 2.50 m of lining material; Sylko; buckle, 40 cm of interlining.

30 Safari suit
4.75 m of 90 cm (2.50 m of 152 cm) fabric for short sleeves; 5.50 m of 90 cm (3 m of 152 cm) fabric for long sleeves; interlining (optional); Sylko; waist elastic or 20 cm zip and waist fastening; buckle; four medium and four or six small buttons.

31 Tunic suit
Fabric as for 30, plus 12 small buttons; a little interlining for collar and cuffs; Sylko; a rouleau leather belt or cord for low, loose belt.

32 Boiler suit
4 m of 90 cm (2 m of 152 cm) fabric; Sylko; 2 cm wide elastic for waist; two buttons; 46-51 cm zip (check your length).

33 Dungarees
3 m of 90 cm (1.70 m of 152 cm) fabric; Sylko; waist elastic, two shoulder strap buckles.

34 Pull-on hat
50 cm of 90 cm (25 cm of 152 cm) stretchy fabric; Sylko.

35 Peaked caps
40 cm of 90 cm fabric; small piece of lining material; Sylko; stiffening for brim; one large button for covering.

36 Fur-trimmed hood
70 cm of 90 cm (70 cm of 152 cm) fabric; the same amount of lining material; Sylko; 2.5 m of 8 cm wide fur or fur fabric.

37 Safari hat
75 cm of 90 cm (50 cm of 152 cm) fabric; small piece of lining; Sylko; stiffening for brim; ribbon for band (optional).

38 Beret
20 cm of 90 cm (20 cm of 152 cm) fabric; the same amount of lining material; Sylko.

39 Spanish hat
70 cm of 90 cm (50 cm of 152 cm) fabric; small piece of lining; 70 cm of stiffening for brim; Sylko; 50 cm of cord.

40 Sun and party dresses
4 m of 90 cm (3.75 m of 152 cm) fabric; Sylko; 36 cm zip; 2.7 m bias binding (b only); ball of very strong crochet cotton for the bobbin thread for gathering (c only).

41 Evening shawl
1 m of 90 cm fabric for a small shawl; 1.25 m of 122 cm fabric for a medium-sized shawl; 1.50 m of 152 cm fabric for a large shawl; Sylko; four times the width of shawl of fringing.

42 Cape
2 m of 138 cm fabric; 2.50 of 90 cm lining material for a short cape; 3 m of 138 cm fabric; 3.70 m of 90 cm lining material for a long cape; 50 cm iron-on Vilene; 60 cm zip; Sylko.

43 'Dorothy' bag
75 cm of 90 cm (50 cm of 152 cm) fabric; small piece of lining; Sylko; length of cord (optional) for drawstrings; piece of cardboard for base.

44 Knitting or work bag
50 cm of 90 cm fabric; Sylko; 40 cm zip; 50 cm of lining.

45 Saddle bag style shoulder bag
70 cm of 90 cm (50 cm of 152 cm) fabric; 70 cm lining material; Sylko; 3 m silk braid for binding; one small buckle for shoulder strap; two split rings; two 20 cm zips.

46 Shoulder bag
70 cm of 90 cm (40 cm of 152 cm) fabric; Sylko; two D-rings; two 36 cm zips; small piece of lining.

47 Shopping bag (1)
70 cm of 90 cm fabric; piece of contrast material for strips; small piece of lining; clothes line to go into handles.

48 Shopping bag (2)
68 x 34 cm piece of canvas about 10-threads to the inch (old measurement); the same amount of lining material; scrap balls of thick wool or embroidery wool of all colours, or bag of 'thrums'.

49 Beach or games bag
1.25 m of 90 cm heavy fabric; the same amount of lining material; strong cotton; 72 cm zip or two half-length ones.

50 'Daisy Jane' rag doll
1 m of 90 cm flesh-coloured stockinette or a dyed T-shirt; one bag of stuffing; one skein of thick black wool for hair; small pieces of felt for features; scrap materials for clothing; Sylko.

51 'Nellie' the elephant
1 m of 122 cm curtain fabric; large bag of stuffing; small pieces of felt; Sylko.

52 'Dracula' the bloodhound
1 m of 90 cm fabric; small squares of felt; one bag of stuffing; Sylko.

53 Toys made with pentagons
Small scraps of fabric or felt; bits of leather; embroidery silk; Sylko; round black beads; pipe cleaners; stuffing.

54 The same oddments as above.

55 The same as 53, plus scraps of long and short fur or fur fabric.

56 The same as 53, plus rice or similar filling.

57 Table-cloth
1.50 x 1.50 m of fabric upwards, according to the length of your table (see diagram); Sylko; lace edging.

58 Place mats
1.40 m of 122 cm furnishing fabric; Sylko.

Index